MW00427173

ARCHITECTS
WHO BUILT
Southern
CALIFORNIA

ANTONIO GONZALEZ

THE
History
PRESS

Published by The History Press
Charleston, SC
www.historypress.com

Copyright © 2019 by Antonio Gonzalez
All rights reserved

First published 2019

Manufactured in the United States

ISBN 9781467141833

Library of Congress Control Number: 2018963524

Notice: The information in this book is true and complete to the best of our knowledge. It is offered without guarantee on the part of the author or The History Press. The author and The History Press disclaim all liability in connection with the use of this book.

All rights reserved. No part of this book may be reproduced or transmitted in any form whatsoever without prior written permission from the publisher except in the case of brief quotations embodied in critical articles and reviews.

CONTENTS

PREFACE

I was unable to locate photographs of O.W. Morgan, W.A.O. Munsell and Philip W. Holler. I did find one of Mendel Meyer but chose not to use it. If anyone related to them has photographs I could use in a future edition of this book, please contact me via my website. If anyone holds the personal papers of any of these architects, I would like to read through them and take notes.

I was interested in writing about architects who hadn't been the subject of much research, so selection was chiefly based on that criteria. Julia Morgan was the exception, but that was because I felt I could add to her scholarship regarding the construction of certain buildings.

I admire all of these architects. Many of them made mistakes during their lives, but what they accomplished far exceeds any of their mistakes. I chose to include the unsavory along with the noteworthy because every time I stumbled upon a new revelation, I read the news accounts wondering why the information wasn't common knowledge to the countless individuals who are fixated, like me, on Southern California architects and their architecture.

I hope *Architects Who Built Southern California* prompts more research into their lives and more books about them.

ACKNOWLEDGEMENTS

I was assisted in this endeavor by a wide variety of people who were extremely helpful. They include Matthew Allnatt, the Jonathan Club; Vinayak Bharne, USC; Pamela Clark, YMCA; Tess Conyers, AC Martin Partners; Kathleen Correia, California State Library; Myles Crowley, MIT; Kendel Darragh, the Library of Michigan; Robert Graef, my lifelong friend; Lambert Giessinger, Los Angeles Department of City Planning; Mike Jones, BPO Elks; Laurie Krill and Abigail Fleming, my wonderful editors at The History Press; Anuja Navare, Pasadena Museum of History; Linda Reed, Stanford Alumni Association; Marccus Reinhardt, California Architects Board; Christina Rice, Los Angeles Public Library; Renato Rodriguez, San Diego History Center; Trudi Sandmeier, USC Heritage Conservation Program; Rio L. Santonil, Al Malaikah Shrine Center; Marcello Vavala, Los Angeles Conservancy; Ruth Wallach, the University of Southern California; Stacy Williams, the University of Southern California; Robert Witney, the Mary Baker Eddy Library; Erin Chase and Steve Hindle, the Huntington Library; Alan Sieroty and Grace Doyle, Sieroty Co.; Tim Strawn and Laura Sorvetti, Cal Poly, San Luis Obispo; Yolanda Bustos, Richard P. Hulser, Brent Riggs and John Cahoon, the Natural History Museum of Los Angeles County; and special thanks to my friend Mark Snowden, who always pointed out when I was acting like a know-it-all, listened to me ramble on about these architects endlessly and gave me feedback regarding this book.

INTRODUCTION

I n 1910, an article appeared in the *Los Angeles Times* titled, "Are Buildings to Go Higher?" Octavius Morgan was the author, and in the piece he addressed the questions of building height and the recent exceptions that had been allowed by city hall. Within the previous few months, the architect of the Alexandria Hotel's annex had requested a variance for the building that included adding thirty feet in height to create a mansard roof. It was allowed. Then, architect A.L. Haley requested and received a variance for the Higgins building, which was under construction at Second and Main Streets. Constructed of reinforced concrete, the Higgins building's height went from 120 feet to 133 feet.

In April 1910, the approved city height for steel-framed buildings was 150 feet and 120 feet for concrete-reinforced buildings.

In the *Times* article, Morgan came out against buildings going higher. He said there was no reason for a congested business district in Los Angeles because there was ample land for expansion east, west and south of the central business district. Morgan also stated there was no river that constrained expansion in any direction, something with which other cities, such as New York, must contend. He asserted that most skyscrapers are built as advertisements for their owners, and most owners have concluded that ten to twelve stories is a profitable height. Morgan continued, noting that even in New York City most large buildings are eight, ten or twelve stories, with some notable exceptions, citing the Metropolitan Life block, which is only eight stories but has a forty-story tower, and the Singer Building, which was twelve stories with a forty-seven-story tower.

The Los Angeles Architectural Club was responsible for yearly architectural exhibits that contained drawings, models and other architectural paraphernalia. Most of the prominent architects in Southern California participated in the exhibitions. *From the* Year Book: Los Angeles Architectural Club, *1913.*

Morgan went on to say that cities like Chicago and New York needed skyscrapers because of the physical conditions of their sites, their enormous populations and their centralized business districts. He could count on one hand the number of beautiful skyscrapers in the United States and listed two that "portend to beauty," citing the Call Building in San Francisco and the Trinity Building in New York as having that quality.

Finally, Morgan said the height of a concrete building is entirely an engineering issue, but he believed eight stories was a safe and profitable limit. The following week, many local architects responded to Morgan's opinion piece in another *Times* column, "The Skyscraper: Morgan Starts a Discussion."

Architect A.L. Haley, who designed the ten-story Higgins building, said more office space would be necessary when the city's population surpassed one million. He stated that office space would have to increase threefold and claimed that the city ordinance limiting the height of reinforced-concrete buildings was discriminatory.

Another architect, Harrison Albright, said the New York skyline resembled a ragged comb with teeth knocked out. He proposed that all of the skyscrapers in Los Angeles be of the same height, making Los Angeles' skyline the most beautiful in the country. He also stated reinforced-concrete buildings could resist severe earthquake shocks more readily.

Alfred Rosenheim, who was president of the Los Angeles Architectural Club, said, "I am opposed to building steel buildings over 150 feet in height and do not approve of either the raising of the steel frame limit by means of the mansard roof to 180 feet or of the recent change permitting reinforced concrete buildings to go to 133 feet."

John Austin, who was one of the men responsible for establishing the limits in the first place, was quoted as saying he stood "pat" on the limits.

Finally, Frank Hudson of Hudson & Munsell, asserted there should be no limit on steel-framed structures: "Los Angeles is going to be as big as any of them. If any man has enough faith in the future of the city to erect a mammoth skyscraper let him, by all means, do it."

1

HARRISON ALBRIGHT

Harrison Albright came to California for the same reason most people come to California—to start a new life—but he didn't move to San Francisco, which was a metropolis even in 1900. Instead, he chose Los Angeles for his new life. At the turn of the twentieth century, Los Angeles was an unruly town with dirt roads and small-scale buildings. Few of the buildings that Albright saw when he arrived in Los Angeles would survive into the twenty-first century. The California Albright moved to no longer exists, but many of the buildings Albright designed have survived, and those buildings have created a bond with the people who inhabit the communities in which the buildings stand and link Californians to a past that has vanished. Albright is important to the architecture of California because in the city of San Diego, where Albright had his biggest impact, the buildings he designed were originally deemed too grandiose for small-town San Diego. John D. Spreckles, one of the titans in San Diego's history, said at a 1923 dinner in his honor,

> *Why did I come to San Diego? Why did any of you come? We came because we thought we saw an unusual opportunity here. We believed that everything pointed to this as the logical site for a great city and seaport. In short, we had faith in San Diego's future, so we cast our lot here. We gave our time and strength and our means to help develop our city, and naturally, our own fortunes. And I, for one, have never lost my first faith in San Diego.*[1]

The film *Field of Dreams* basically said the same thing with these seven words: "If you build it, they will come," and they did. Many of the key buildings that are the foundation for the city of San Diego, that give it its inherit character, are Harrison Albright buildings.

Albright was born in Shoemakertown, Pennsylvania, on May 17, 1866. His parents were Joseph and Louise (née Jeannot), and he had two elder sisters, Alice and Emma, which made Harrison the youngest in the family. He attended local public schools, the Pierce College of Business and the Spring Garden Institute, but there is no evidence that he received a degree in architecture or engineering.

Albright opened an architectural office in Philadelphia in 1886, and it remained opened until 1891, when he married Susie J. Bemus. The couple would eventually have three children—Anna Louise, Catherine and Harrison Jr.—but first, he and his wife

Harrison Albright acquired a great deal of wealth, but at the end of his life he was unable to enjoy the benefits of his success. *Courtesy of Greater Los Angeles & Southern California Portraits & Personal Memoranda.*

moved to Charleston, West Virginia, where he opened another office and remained in business there from 1891 to 1905. Albright designed two buildings of some note before he arrived in Los Angeles in 1905: the annex for the capitol in Charleston and the West Baden Springs Hotel in Indiana. The West Baden Springs Hotel (1902) was referred to as "the eighth wonder of the world" during its heyday, and while it was abandoned from 1983 to 1996 and put on *Preservation* magazine's "endangered list," it was saved by the Historic Landmark Foundation of Indiana and is no longer threatened. It is likely U.S. Grant Jr. saw one or both buildings and they were the basis for Harrison Albright's selection for the U.S. Grant Hotel. At the very least, Grant knew of them—it seems improbable that Albright would have arrived in Los Angeles as an unknown and within months acquired a huge commission from Grant to design the landmark U.S. Grant Hotel.

U.S. GRANT HOTEL

It was on May 10, 1905, that the *Los Angeles Times* reported San Diego's Horton House hotel, built in 1872, would be demolished and a new hotel would be erected in its place. The man behind the new hotel was Ulysses S. Grant Jr., the former president's son. Demolition was set to commence in July 1905, and while Grant was being urged to name the hotel after his father, he favored naming the new hotel after the old one.

Yet it took more than five years for the building to be completed from the time it was originally announced. Harrison Albright had estimated it would take a year to build, but it didn't open until October 15, 1910. The principal reason for the slow progress was Grant's failure to raise enough cash for the building's construction prior to the groundbreaking. Grant had continual problems throughout the construction of the building—all due to lack of money.

Grant originally found funding with the National Sureties Company and later acquired more capital through Colonel A.G. Gassen and Ralph Granger. Gassen bought certain properties Grant owned in the San Diego area, which provided Grant with ready cash. Granger invested $350,000

U.S. Grant Hotel. According to the *Weekly Union* newspaper, the hotel's prominent features were its perfect lines and "gigantic massiveness." *Courtesy of* American Architect.

that he obtained from the sale of property he owned in Brooklyn, New York. During construction, though, the U.S. Grant Hotel was a money pit. When Carl Leonardt, the Los Angeles contractor who received the concrete contract, wasn't paid in a timely manner, Leonardt sued for failure to provide payment. Lawsuits were then filed by numerous parties connected with the construction, and all work ceased. What followed over the subsequent years were long periods of time when no work was done on the hotel. It sat on Broadway, between Third and Fourth Avenues, in a state of incompleteness. As year after year passed, the citizens of San Diego viewed any announcement regarding the resumption of construction on the hotel with skepticism.

This was not Albright's only project during this period. In 1906, Albright designed and saw to completion, in an industrial area of Los Angeles, the Santa Fe Freight House for the Santa Fe Railroad. This building still stands in an altered configuration, with the dock area enclosed, and is now used by the architectural school SCI-ARC as its main building. In the following year, 1907, Albright designed the Spreckels mansion for John D. Spreckels in Coronado. Coronado was a tony suburb of San Diego, and the Spreckels mansion was on the market in 2017 for $15.9 million. Spreckels must have liked Albright because he would later hire him for two other large San Diego commissions: the Union Tribune Building and the Spreckels Office

The Spreckels mansion. *From* The Man: John D. Spreckels.

and Theater complex. But before either of those was erected, 1907 saw one other major building from Albright—the Consolidated Realty Building on the corner of Sixth and Hill Streets in downtown Los Angeles. It wouldn't be finished until 1910, but this wasn't due to lack of funding.

In September 1908, Grant found another financial backer by the name of Hulett Clinton Merritt, a "well-known capitalist"[2] and real estate investor from Pasadena. Merritt was originally from Minnesota and helped create the Lake Superior Consolidated Iron Mines, also known as the Merritt-Rockefeller syndicate. In 1901, Merritt and Rockefeller sold their holdings to U.S. Steel for $81 million. When Merritt invested money (pocket change for him) in the Grant Hotel project, he did it to help his friend, not U.S. Grant, but rather John H. Holmes, who was also from Pasadena.

Merritt enjoyed investing in real estate. In the panic of 1907, Merritt bought two of the best corners in downtown Los Angeles, according to *Notables of Southwest*, so he had enough spare cash to gamble on Holmes. John H. Holmes, who had worked at the Green Hotel in Pasadena for nineteen years, would eventually lease the Grant Hotel from the owners and was referred to in one newspaper account as "the commander in chief" of the Grant Hotel.

In the spring of 1909, it looked like the hotel might never be finished. Claims against the corporation behind the hotel hovered around $80,000, and construction was at a standstill. In June 1909, Leonardt was in court suing for $140,000 he claimed was owed him. Grant countered by alleging that Leonardt's work was unfinished and in some places substandard. Grant also alleged "that the contractor [Leonardt] entered into collusion with Harrison Albright, the defendant's architect, to reengineer the building and to change the specifications agreed to by plaintiff and defendant."[3]

Grant's accusations did not hurt Albright's reputation, as this was not Albright's only project. His other buildings went up without any complications or delays. The Consolidated Realty Building took three

Carl Leonardt was the contractor for the Los Angeles County Hall of Records, U.S. Grant Hotel, the (old) Orpheum Theater in Los Angeles, the Pacific Electric Building, the Hotel Green in Pasadena and the Hamburger Building. *Courtesy of* Notables of the Southwest.

years to build but only because more floors were added during construction as the Sixth and Hill location became more desirable to potential tenants.

In July 1910, it was reported in the *San Diego Union* that Grant

> *feels what he regards as a lack of interest in the hotel project on a part of a number of businessmen in San Diego. It is said he told an intimate friend before leaving the city last Saturday that he was much disappointed in the reception of his cherished scheme by the better class of business men of San Diego and by the failure of the public in general to appreciate the importance of the big hostelry's relation to the upbuilding of the municipality.*[4]

At this point, Louis J. Wilde entered the picture. Wilde was born in Iowa City, Iowa, arrived in Los Angeles in 1884 and moved to San Diego in 1903. He was president of San Diego's American National Bank and responsible for who stayed and who left the project. Albright stayed on as architect, and Wilde convinced Grant to turn over the construction of the hotel to a board of trustees—a board of which he was president. The board of trustees became promoters of the project, and the banks that the trustees represented sold bonds to raise the capital to finish the hotel. Grant seemed to lose interest in the venture soon after he transferred control of the project. Yet he really had no choice. If he hadn't agreed to Wilde's plan, it is likely the hotel would have been put into receivership and Grant would have ended up bankrupt.

Wilde's concern for the project could have been based in alleviating the huge eyesore that sat in the center of downtown. As a leader in the small community, Wilde may have felt obligated to take charge of the problem and relieve the city of the embarrassment that Grant's incompetence had created, but Wilde could have seen it as an opportunity too—to swoop in and take control of a project that, when completed, would generate a great deal of money as the city of San Diego grew.

Grant received $1 million in mortgage bonds for his stake. In the summer of 1910, the *Los Angeles Times* reported, "Mr. Grant has severed all connection with the costly hotel that bears his name, and that a new corporation, known as the U.S. Grant Hotel and Office Building Company, has taken over the valuable property. Mr. Grant has no connection with this company, though it bears his name."[5]

Los Angeles' Barker Brothers received the contract to furnish the hotel. The contract included furnishings for all 437 rooms, including the public spaces, along with linens, glassware and silver. The furniture cost was estimated to be in the $200,000 range, though the final cost was $250,000. The contract was hammered out by an agent representing the hotel's owners; the hotel's lessee, John H. Holmes; and a Barker Brothers representative, W.A. Barker.

Then, on October 1, 1910, Louis J. Wilde acquired a 50 percent stake in the hotel. The *Evening Tribune* wrote,

> *The entire arrangement will work a benefit for all interests in the big establishment. It puts the hotel bonds on a perfectly sound basis. It preserves Mr. Grant's personal estate which it is said was in jeopardy and would have been sold at a great loss to meet claims. It puts the operating company on a firm footing and generally places the hotel in an excellent condition for the formal opening.*[6]

The official grand opening took place on October 15, 1910, with over six hundred invited guests. U.S. Grant Jr. did not attend the event. Instead, he sent a telegram to Wilde: "My congratulations on your completing and successfully opening Grant Hotel. Hope honors will be accorded you for stupendous work, finished against great difficulties and opposition which disheartened me."[7]

Mr. and Mrs. Wilde were the first individuals to sign the guest book, and then a signed slip of paper with U.S. Grant Jr.'s signature was pasted in.

It is unclear why Harrison Albright was not included in any of the extensive newspaper lists of opening night attendees, but it doesn't appear Albright attended the event. He may have been exhausted from the project and glad it was over. The difficult memories he had of the building's construction and the accusations by Grant may have made the decision not to attend an easy one.

Originally, the hotel had 420 guest rooms. It also had 8 bridal suites on the second floor, and the ballroom on the ninth floor could accommodate 1,200. The final cost of constructing the building was $1.1 million. The value of the land was placed at $600,000, so the total cost, including the Barker Brothers furnishings, was $1.95 million. Other points of interest: there were 500 telephones in the building, four passenger elevators and four freight elevators. There were two separate pools in the basement, one for men and one for women. The estimated cost of running the hotel, every day, was $1,000, and it employed 250 people. A large oil painting of former president Ulysses S. Grant was hung over the main staircase in a place of honor. Most architectural historians classify the U.S. Grant Hotel as early twentieth-century, Beaux-Arts, classical revival style.

U.S. Grant Hotel lobby. On opening night, there was a huge crush of people to check in. Most waited patiently, while others went to one of the hotel's cafés for a drink. *Author's collection.*

A postcard view of the Bivouac Room. *Author's collection.*

The only other hotel of any comparison in the San Diego area would have been the Hotel del Coronado, which was built in 1888 as a resort. The Hotel del Coronado had over seven hundred rooms, but the Grant Hotel wasn't a resort. The Grant Hotel was for travelers and businessmen.

The Consolidated Realty Building, begun in 1907, was completed in 1910, and the *Los Angeles Times* praised the design: "The building, which was designed by Harrison Albright, is a monument to the progress of the streets upon which it is situated and of the growth of the city itself."[8] Originally, the building was slated to be two stories with a foundation that could support many more floors, but as the building's location became highly desirable, more floors were added until the building topped out at six stories. In December 1909, when almost finished, the builders decided to add three more floors because the University Club stated it would rent out floors eight and nine, if built, and sign a ten-year lease, too. Said the *Times*, "The general prosperity of the city led the builders to alter their plans."[9]

As the Consolidated Realty Building's construction concluded, in November 1910—a month after the Grant Hotel's opening, Harrison Albright announced the construction of the six-story Spreckels Office Building and Theater. It would be a reinforced-concrete building with a theater and occupy an entire block in San Diego, fronting D Street (Broadway) between First and Second Avenues. When it was originally announced, only the theater section, which was in the center of the building, was to be six stories; the adjoining office sections, on both sides, were designed to be two stories. However, in the final plans, the entire office building was six stories.

SPRECKELS THEATER AND OFFICE BUILDING

John Diedrich Spreckels, the man behind the building, was listed as a "capitalist" in many publications from the first decades of the twentieth century. (This was a common term used for businessmen with enough money to invest in large commercial real estate projects.) He was born on August 16, 1853, in Charleston, South Carolina, and attended Oakland College and Germany's Polytechnic School. Spreckels studied chemistry and mechanical engineering and moved to San Diego in 1887. He owned many businesses, including newspapers. A short list would include the Oceanic Steamship Company, Spreckels Sugar, the *San Diego Union*, the *Evening Tribune*, Coronado Water Company and the Hotel del Coronado. Spreckels didn't necessarily have an interest in theaters, but he did have an interest in being a civic booster and providing San Diego with the amenities that would help it grow. Spreckels built the city's streetcar lines with his own money and stated he always invested his money in new projects to protect the money he had already invested in previous projects: "Well, the aim of my life has been the building up of San Diego. Men like me get our reward in the very activity of doing, or of trying to do, big things. It is my life."[10]

The office building took two years to complete, and the stated cost for the land and the building was reported to be $1 million. When it was completed, the six-story office building was the largest in the city of San Diego. The theater opened on August 22, 1912, with a show called *Bought and Paid For*; it was brought from New York but scheduled to play at the theater for only two days. On Sunday, August 25, a Gilbert and Sullivan festival began with performances of *The Mikado*, *The Pirates of Penzance* and *H.M.S. Pinafore*. For the theater's first season, the other productions booked included the Metropolitan Opera, female impersonator Julian Eltinge and Dustin Farnum in *The Littlest Rebel*.

John Spreckels requested the theater have 1,915 seats to commemorate the year San Diego would host the Panama-California Exposition. When built, the auditorium was seventy-two feet deep by eighty-eight feet wide. The stage was eighty-eight feet wide by fifty-two feet deep. The walls and ceilings of the lobby, box office, elevator recess and staircases were all finished in Pedara onyx from Mexico. The *San Diego Union* reported the plasterwork in the theater was "highly decorated in the most lavish manner consistent with good taste."[11] There were no pillars to mar views because the balcony was suspended from the load-bearing walls with the aid of huge steel beams. Surprisingly, a great deal of newspaper text was devoted to the theater and lobby lighting, and "the refined glow of electric lights" was much written about and made possible because of "the rapid development of the past few years in electrical science."[12] The painting above the proscenium arch depicts Neptune in a chariot bringing prosperity to San Diego. The allegorical paintings in the ceiling's domes depict *Dawn*, *Air*, *Earth*, *Water* and *Fire* painted by Emil T. Mazy of Los Angeles. When the theater opened, a large basement under the theater contained an orchestra pit, a stage pit, dressing rooms, toilets, a restaurant and a kitchen. The restaurant was accessible from D Street through two large staircases.

The *San Diego Union* pointed out that behind all the attractive interior theater decoration was not a "flimsy pine framework inviting a torch of flame to create instantly an awful deathtrap"[13] but instead walls, beams

Spreckels Theater and Office Building. The new theater was seen as an advertisement for the city and an attraction for winter tourists. *From the* Year Book: Los Angeles Architectural Club, *1911.*

and ceilings made of concrete. The newspaper stressed that the theater came equipped with "six independent side exit doors equipped with panic bolts to open outward with the slightest pressure from within."[14] It also had automatic sprinklers above the stage and a "curtain of steel" lined with vitrified asbestos that could be lowered in twenty seconds to keep the audience safe from any fire on the stage.

Architect Irving Gill attended the theater's opening and stated,

> *The acoustics of the auditorium leave nothing to be striven for by builders of the future, further than a reproduction of the effects produced here. It would be a great benefit especially for architects if the world's greatest authority on acoustics could come to San Diego and make a study of this auditorium and write critical analysis of its structure. I extend congratulations to architect Albright on the results he has accomplished.*[15]

Harrison Albright proclaimed on opening day, "San Diego makes another long stride towards metropolitan distinction with the opening of the Spreckels Theater tonight."[16]

John Spreckels was frequently accused of trying to turn San Diego into his own personal town. *From* The Man: John D. Spreckels.

The population of San Diego grew rapidly from seventeen thousand in 1900 to fifty thousand in 1912—more than a threefold increase. It was a new town and seemed to be suffering from an inferiority complex from what can be gleaned from the *Evening Tribune*. The newspaper quoted John Spreckels the day before the theater opened:

> *Too many of us think of it as ahead of the town just as we thought of the U.S. Grant Hotel. Just so, it is not ahead of the town; the town is ready for it now, needs it and its growth has been hampered without it. Let's get that fixed in our minds; the Spreckels Theater is none too big and none too good for San Diego right now.*[17]

In 1915, Albright lived at 618 South Benton Way in Los Angeles, and his office was in the Laughlin Building, which was located at 315 South Broadway, also in Los Angeles. By 1930, the family had moved to 708 Imperial Avenue in San Diego. Before he retired, Albright was described in a 1921 article in the *Los Angeles Herald* as a wealthy property owner with extensive real estate holdings in Los Angeles and San Diego Counties. At that time, his family filed a petition stating that he was incompetent to manage his affairs and requested the Title Insurance and Trust Company be appointed as guardian of his estate.

In a letter to the Albright's land agent, Colonel Ed Fletcher, from Woodruff & Shoemaker, attorneys and counselors at law, dated May 3, 1922, the law firm wrote: "As you have been informed, Mr. Albright has been declared incompetent and the Title Insurance and Trust Company appointed the guardian of his estate."[18] Susie Albright wrote to Fletcher too and said, "My husband has been under the care of one of the oldest and best brain specialists in this city and has improved very much during the past week."[19] Albright officially retired from his practice in 1925 and was listed as an invalid in the 1930 census. He died on January 3, 1932. He was survived by his wife, Susie, and his children, Anna Louise, Catherine and Harrison Jr.

JOHN AUSTIN

John Austin spent more than fifty years designing buildings in the Los Angeles area. Early in his career, he designed the Potter Hotel in Santa Barbara (1903) with Myron Hunt. Austin went on to design a Carnegie Library in Anaheim (1909) and NBC Studios in Hollywood (1938), and in a partnership with three other architectural firms, he worked on the Superior Court House of California (1958). His three biggest jobs remain Los Angeles landmarks and are part of the landscape that defines the city.

John Corneley Wilson Austin was born on February 13, 1870, in Bodicote, England. His parents were Richard Wilson Austin and Jane Elizabeth Austin. He attended private schools but did not attend any college or university and never received a degree in architecture, engineering or any other related field. He did receive architectural training while working for architect William S. Barwick in England. Austin moved to the United States in 1891 and lived in Philadelphia and San Francisco before moving to Los Angeles in 1895.

Austin's first wife was between eight and ten years older than Austin, depending on the source consulted. Census records indicate she married Austin in 1890, and they had one daughter, Dorothy, who was born in 1891. Her *Los Angeles Herald* obituary from November 23, 1901, stated that "Mrs. Louisa E. Austin wife of John C. Austin [died] at the California hospital in Los Angeles yesterday, as the result of an operation." Her *Times* obituary elaborated, "Mrs. Austin was prominent and popular in musical circles of Los Angeles, and recently was elected secretary of the Treble Clef Club."

At her funeral, four members of the local American Institute of Architects branch acted as pallbearers, and the music was supplied by the Treble Clef Club. Austin's second marriage, to Hilda Myttoon, was announced in the *Los Angeles Herald* on August 19, 1902. The ceremony was held at 611 West Eleventh Street, which was the home of the bride's mother. The Reverend Dr. Wilkins, from a local Episcopal church, performed the ceremony in front of a small group of family members. "The bride wore a neat fawn-colored traveling suit and walking hat to match."[20] The couple went to San Francisco for their honeymoon and returned to Los Angeles to reside on Sherman Street.

Austin had seven children with his second wife, Hilda: Marjorie, Gwendolen, William, Violet, Angela, Harold and Phyllis. According to *Notables of the Southwest*, "By the first marriage there is one child, Dorothy Austin."[21]

In 1910, Austin was involved in a train crash when a freight train hauling lumber backed into a Pasadena-bound electric trolley car. The trolley, which was filled with people, was lifted up and thrown fifteen feet due to the speed and force of the freight train. The trolley landed on its side. Austin survived with a bruised left eye and cuts on his face and body. He was traveling with W.A.O. Munsell from the firm Hudson & Munsell. Munsell also survived, but he suffered numerous hand and leg lacerations.

Austin was president of the Southern California chapter of the American Institute of Architects in 1912 and president of the Los Angeles Humane Society for Children in 1913.[22] He also worked to have the AIA convention in California in 1915. Austin was considered one of Los Angeles' major architects, and he was viewed as a "go to" person to speak for the architectural community. In an article titled "The Profession of Architecture," published in the magazine *Architect and Engineer*, Austin wrote about his vision of an architect:

> *An architect is not, as some think, a glorified contractor who makes pictures. Usually, he is a man of education, business ability and resource, who is called upon to solve large problems and adjust petty difficulties almost in the same breath. He is called upon to spend great sums of money in such a manner that it will bring a substantial return to the owner. He must design a building that will not make the neighbors curse the day of his birth, and he must embody all of the latest appliances for comfort that he knows of—and some that he doesn't.*[23]

The Potter Hotel burned to the ground in two hours. *Author's collection.*

By 1925, Austin had been a working architect in Los Angeles for over twenty years, and while he was well respected and made a living building local libraries, schools and banks, he had not designed any truly monumental buildings—with the exception of the Potter Hotel, which burned to the ground in 1921. A trio of buildings Austin designed over the next decade ensured his legacy. Thompson Mayes wrote in a series of articles titled "Why Do Old Places Matter" that one of the reasons people gravitate toward certain buildings is because they instill civic identity. Austin's three major buildings tap into this idea of civic identity.

THE SHRINE AUDITORIUM

The first building in Austin's trio was the Shrine Auditorium, completed in 1926.

Shriners are Masons, and all Shriners have to be Masons before they can become Shriners. In 1920, the Shrine temple located at Jefferson and Royal Streets was destroyed by fire. The construction of a new Shrine auditorium and temple (temples are now called Shrine centers) was scheduled to rise on the site of the old temple according to an announcement given on October 17, 1921, by Potentate Louis M. Cole. (A potentate is the leader of the Shrine and oversees the Shrine's business.) The new Shrine auditorium would seat seven thousand and cost around $1 million. *Al Malaikah*, which is Arabic for "the angels," was the name that would be given to the temple. In the months after the fire, the Shriners acquired more land adjacent to the burnt temple, so they owned a large portion of the entire block.

The auditorium, the largest west of the Mississippi, would be situated south of downtown on Royal and Jefferson Streets with the front of the building facing Royal. The stage would measure 192 feet by 72 feet with all the accompanying necessities, including dressing rooms and a fly system. The recently acquired

John Austin. *Courtesy of Greater Los Angeles & Southern California Portraits & Personal Memoranda.*

land, nearer to Thirty-Second Street, would be the location of a ballroom and banquet room along with meeting rooms for the Shriners.

The Al Malaikah Building Corporation was formed to finance the building, and stock was sold to raise the money. It was hoped the entire amount could be raised from Shrine members. John Austin and A.M. Edelman were announced as the architects of the job, and according to news reports, the two men had been working on the plans for months. The groundbreaking was scheduled for January 1922.

The invitations for the groundbreaking went out on August 25, 1922. The delay was due to a ballot referendum put before Los Angeles voters regarding a public auditorium, which was defeated. With that loss, the Shriners realized they would be able to rent out their auditorium to non-Shriners for public events throughout the year and enlarged the project. The groundbreaking took place on September 2 at 11:00 a.m., and the ceremony was filmed "for the motion picture history of the temple."

According to the *Times*, it was designed in the Sarascenic (Saracenic) style, which is found in India, the Holy Land, Spain, North Africa and Turkey.[24]

Three years and four months later, on January 13, 1926, former potentate Louis M. Cole unveiled the building for the press and civic leaders. It was an architectural marvel in many ways. The building had a frontage of 150 feet by 250 feet. At the time, it contained the largest stage in the world, with a square footage of 13,800. The proscenium was 100 feet wide by 36 feet high. Total seating was 6,550, with 3,200 seats on the main floor and 3,350 seats in the balcony. There was an asbestos and reinforced steel drop curtain that weighed twenty-three tons and the main chandelier weighed almost five tons. The chandelier, comprising over 100,000 individual pieces of glass, is twenty feet in diameter and over twenty-eight feet in length. It is wired with 500 light sockets and most fitted with 150-watt bulbs. The chandelier uses 62,445 watts when completely lit.

A single 168-foot-long truss weighing 255 tons supports the entire balcony. The building is constructed of reinforced concrete and structural steel and cost $2.5 million. In the Shriners' publication *A Civic Need Fulfilled*, which was published at the time of the building's opening, only John Austin was listed as the architect. The publication also mentioned facts about the roof: "The domed roof, which measures 192 feet across its arch, weighs 1,870 tons. Six steel trusses, each 28 feet high by 198 feet long and weighing 60 tons each, support the roof. One end of each of these trusses rests on free moving steel rollers to allow for possible expansion and contraction of the

The Shriners moved into the building in 1926, and it is still used and owned by the Shriners. *Author photo.*

concrete roof."[25] The *Los Angeles Times* described the entrance: "The main entrance to the building, fronting Royal Street, is through five pointed arches, surmounted by a richly decorated arcade, in the manner of the early Mahometan mosques, and flanked at the corners by twin domed turrets, carrying at their apices the crescent, the scimitar and the star."[26]

The 1954 Judy Garland film *A Star Is Born* was filmed at the Shrine. The stage was also used in conjunction with the filming of the 1933 version of *King Kong*. Both Frank Sinatra and Jimi Hendrix have performed on the Shrine Stage.

The Shrine was declared Los Angeles Cultural Heritage Monument No. 139 on March 5, 1975.

LOS ANGELES CITY HALL

The second building that ensures Austin's place in Los Angeles architectural history is Los Angeles City Hall (1928). He designed this building in collaboration with two other Los Angeles architects, Albert C. Martin and John Parkinson, but the job almost went to another firm, and Austin, Martin and Parkinson refused to take themselves out of the running when the firm originally selected offered a compromise that would have awarded the commission to another, altruistic group of architects.

Aleck Curlett and Claud Beelman were the architects selected to design Los Angeles' new city hall by the city council on February 19, 1925. When informed of their selection, Curlett said it was completely unexpected.[27]

President of the city council Boyle Workman stated on the day of the announcement that the council wanted to select an established architectural firm for the new city hall project but was against hiring the Allied Architects or "the independents.[28] The independents Workman alluded to were John Austin, Albert C. Martin and John Parkinson, who would refer to themselves as the Associated Architects. The Allied Architects group was founded in 1921 for the advancement of public architecture. When the Allied Architects group was formed, Octavius Morgan, O.W. Morgan, Edwin Bergstrom, Elmer Grey and Myron Hunt were all members. According to *Southwest Builder and Contractor*, the Allied Architects were "to provide municipal, county, state and national governments with the highest and best expression of the art of architecture in designing, planning and construction of public buildings, structures and improvements and at the least possible cost."[29]

Hidden behind the Allied Architects stated purpose was that the group didn't want any local city and county work awarded to architectural firms from other parts of the country.

Claud Beelman said after the selection that they made no effort to obtain the contract and they didn't expect to receive it, but now that they had it, they would immediately get to work on the plans.[30]

Thirteen days later, the city council voted to direct the city attorney to compel the Board of Public Works to hire Curlett and Beelman. The Board of Public Works felt it, and it alone, could select the architects, and the board had no intention of hiring Curlett and Beelman. Its choices were John C. Austin, Albert C. Martin and John Parkinson. When the Board of Public Works failed to sign Curlett and Beelman, the city council, on March 7, decided to draw up a contract and have Curlett and Beelman sign the document.

Mayor George E. Cryer (1921–29) felt he was the only person who should sign any contract drawn up by the city council, yet his opinion was being ignored by both the Board of Public Works and the city council. Arthur Eldridge of the Board of Public Works said he thought the contract was invalid so he would never vote to authorize payment.[31] While it was unclear if the city council could hire the architects under the existing city charter, under the new city charter, which became effective on July 1, 1925, it was clear that only the Board of Public Works could hire the architects. One councilman, Robert M. Allan, said he felt the board might tie up the issue in the courts until after July 1. On March 10, 1925, an injunction was granted by a Los Angeles court that prevented the council from hiring Curlett and Beelman. It had already done so, but on August 4, 1925, the city council contract was deemed invalid.

Curlett and Beelman said they would walk away from the deal if Austin, Martin and Parkinson would take themselves out of the competition and let the Allied Architects have the commission. Curlett and Beelman were reaching out and trying to offer a solution that would ensure "good will" among the local architectural community, but Austin, Martin and Parkinson were rather ruthless. They listened, but they didn't step aside. Curlett and Beelman threatened to sue the city for their "supposed profits," but they declined to pursue any court action. One possibility is that they didn't pursue legal action because they realized they would never receive any future city work if they did sue.

On August 17, 1925, Austin, Martin and Parkinson were officially employed by the city, and the city council authorized a $10,000 payment to the architects for the preliminary plans on September 23, 1925. The building had a $5 million cost estimate, and the contract the city signed stipulated the architects would receive a 6 percent payment of the final cost of the finished building, or $270,000 to $300,000.

On September 25, 1925, the board received the architects' plans, which specified that the building would be twenty-eight stories high and rise to 430 feet. The height was designed to accommodate twenty years of growth, and the building would have 424 feet of frontage along Spring Street with a depth of 240 feet. It was designed in the Italian Renaissance style over a steel frame. In a statement released by the architects timed to correspond with the building's announcement, the Associated Architects' stated, "The monumental character of the new Los Angeles City Hall will be obtained almost entirely by means of silhouette, architectural form and scale. Decoration will be confined to the lower stories of the exterior, where it may be easily seen and appreciated by the public."[32] The three lower floors would be covered in granite while the upper floors would be covered in terra cotta.

A myth that most transplants to Southern California hear when they begin to learn about Los Angeles architecture is that, for decades, no building could be taller than city hall and laws were enforced to prevent any building from exceeding city hall's height. That's not true. The truth is an exception was made for the new city hall.

One of the issues discussed when the plans were approved was the 430-foot tower. A height limit of 150 feet had been in place since 1905 for structural safety reasons, possibly, but it has never been clear why the 150-foot limit was enacted and those responsible have all died. New fire laws were instituted around 1905, so that's a possibility too. Regardless of the reason, the new city hall's tower would need an exception to the law. Council members, President Boyle Workman and Mayor Cryer agreed that the exception should be put before voters in the form of a referendum. All felt the public would approve the height exception, and it was scheduled to be put on the ballot as Proposition No. 7, but the public didn't have to vote. A "friendly" lawsuit was filed by one of the contractors in court to determine if the city could build a public building more than 150 feet tall. The friendly lawsuit involved Hugh J. McGuire, who was president of the Los Angeles Board of Public Works, and his refusal to sign the contract with the firm selected to construct the building, the C.J. Kubach Company. The Kubach Company immediately filed suit and demanded the contract be signed. McGuire stated in newspaper accounts that he didn't sign the contract deliberately to trigger court action and expedite a decision regarding the height limit law.

On August 9, 1926, the California Supreme Court decided Los Angeles could build its 430-foot city hall.

In a book published to commemorate the building, its architecture was described in symbolic terms:

> *The three salient features of the building may be compared to the characteristics of the city which it serves—the broad and solid base is typical of the City's firm foundation at the strategic point of the great Southwest; the flanking wings rising from the base typify its marvelous growth from the original pueblo; while the soaring lines of the tower symbolize the indomitable spirit of its citizens that made it possible. May it endure so that future generations shall benefit from what their forefathers have wrought.*[33]

The groundbreaking took place on March 4, 1926; the foundation was started on May 7, 1926; and the erection of the steel frame commenced on July 24, 1926.

Ten months later, a parade to commemorate the laying of the cornerstone took place on Wednesday, June 22, 1927. By this date, the steel frame had been finished, twelve floors of concrete had been poured, a quarter of the granite had been placed on the lower three floors of the building and the building was considered half finished. The parade began at the old city hall on Broadway, built in 1888, with Mayor Cryer and Governor C.C. Young. The parade proceeded up Broadway to the courthouse and hall of records, where county officials joined it. The procession turned right on Temple Street, proceeded down to Spring Street and turned right again, stopping in front of the new city hall. A police escort and the firemen's band led the parade. The parade route was approximately five blocks.

A grandstand with two thousand seats was erected in front of the main city hall entrance for invited guests. The Native Sons of the Golden West performed the cornerstone ritual. Inside the cornerstone were placed newspapers from that day, a printed list of city officials, a photograph of Mayor Cryer, a copy of the city charter and coins minted from California gold. Speaking at the event were Governor Young, Mayor Cryer and President McGarry of the chamber of commerce. It was noted in newspaper accounts that the architects of the building would be introduced at the ceremony.

In September 1927, a call went out for donations to fund the Lindbergh Beacon, which was scheduled to be erected atop city hall. The Lindbergh Beacon was a high-powered light that was attached to the very top of city

NEW LOS ANGELES CITY HALL
JOHN C. AUSTIN, ALBERT C. MARTIN, JOHN PARKINSON
Associate Architects

C. J. KUBACH CO., General Contractors

Postcard with the new city hall. *Courtesy of Mark Snowden.*

hall and rotated. It was designed to alert aircraft of the building's presence and commemorate Charles Lindbergh's historic flight. The film director Cecil B. DeMille had contributed the first $100 to the fund, but the amount raised was less than $1,000 of the $3,000 needed. As the new city hall came closer to being finished, there was a discussion about what to do with the old city hall. Mayor Cryer wanted to sell the building, but when the old city hall was appraised at only $585,000, Cryer and the city council were unsure of how to proceed. The building was seen as a liability to any sale because it would cost a great deal to demolish.

On March 26, 1928, the Board of Public Works accepted the new city hall building through a resolution and terminated the contract with the architects. The board's resolution stated, "The architects are commended by this board for the eminently satisfactory and beautiful design of the monumental building and for the efficiency displayed by them in supervising the erection of the building so that it was completed expeditiously and economically."[34]

Joseph M. Schenck, president of United Artists and one of the future heads of 20th Century Fox, was put in charge of the Citizen's Dedication Committee. This committee oversaw every aspect of the building's dedication and opening, which took place over a three-day period beginning on April 26, 1928. A parade took place on the first day and included twenty-six bands along with marching groups that included the U.S. Army, U.S. Navy, National Guard, military schools, Boy Scouts and various veteran groups. All passed in front of the reviewing stand at city hall. Also included on opening day was a luncheon at the Biltmore Hotel for five hundred visiting city leaders from throughout the state and a flag raising ceremony. Money was found so the Lindbergh Beacon was lit by President Calvin Coolidge, who did this by pressing a golden button in the Oval Office three thousand miles away. A night aerial circus, in honor of Charles Lindbergh, was performed, and there were fireworks. The public was allowed to enter the new city hall starting at 7:30 p.m.

Los Angeles City Hall was declared Los Angeles Historic Cultural Monument No. 150 on March 24, 1976.

Austin was held in the highest esteem after the city hall's completion. He was elected president of the Los Angeles Chamber of Commerce in 1930 and recruited in 1931 to coordinate unemployment relief in ten southern California counties, including Los Angeles County, during the Great Depression. He was asked to perform this task by Walter S. Gifford, who was the national head of President Franklin Delano Roosevelt's organization for unemployment relief.

Chandelier in Los Angeles City Hall's rotunda. *Courtesy of the California History Room, California State Library, Sacramento, California.*

Austin's second wife, Hilda, died in 1931. In 1935, Austin did something unusual when he was sixty-three years old; he married his adoptive daughter Dorothy K. Austin. Newspaper reports stated Dorothy was the niece of his first wife and had been Austin's ward since the time she was two. Miss Austin, who was then forty-three, was an employee of Compton Junior High School, where she was head of the English department.

On Sunday, February 3, 1935, Austin alerted the press to a change in his wedding plans. While he and his adoptive daughter still planned on getting married at Pasadena's All Saints Episcopal Church, the Reverend Leslie E. Learned, who performed the wedding service for five of Austin's children, was ill and wouldn't be able to perform the ceremony for Austin and his bride.

The wedding did take place, and the Reverend Francis Foote performed the ceremony. The *Los Angeles Times* had a photograph of the couple between two headlines. The top headline said, "Newlyweds on Honeymoon." The bottom headline said, "John C. Austin, architect, weds adopted daughter." In the photograph, the bride is wearing a dark coat with a fur-lined collar and a hat with large feathers, and she's holding a bouquet of flowers. Austin is wearing a suit and wire-rimmed eyeglasses. He looks portly. Both are smiling.

Only family members attended the service. After the wedding ceremony, the couple departed on an "automobile honeymoon to the south."[35]

GRIFFITH OBSERVATORY

Colonel Griffith was a pariah when he died due to the prison term he served for assault with the intent to commit murder. Griffith and his wife were staying at the Arcadia Hotel in Santa Monica during the summer of 1903, and it was in this hotel that Mrs. Griffith was shot. Colonel Griffith stated that he returned to the hotel on the evening of September 3 to find his wife packing because the two had agreed to leave the next day and travel back to Los Angeles. Seeing what his wife was doing, Griffith started to tinker about the room, "folding up clothing of my own and doing other little things of that sort."[36] While he was doing this, for some reason, his wife was packing his revolver in her trunk and it accidently went off and shot her in the face. She cried out, "I am hurt,"[37] became hysterical, ran to the window and somehow fell out. The Griffiths were staying in a room on the third floor, and Mrs. Griffith fell to the roof of the second floor. She summoned the strength to climb into a second-floor window and found sanctuary there. When she could tell her side of the story, it was different from his. She said Colonel Griffith came back to the room late on September 3, intoxicated. He was in a rage and, with his revolver in his hand, told his wife, "Get your prayer book and kneel down and cover your eyes. I'm going to shoot you and I'm going to kill you."[38] She pleaded with her husband, saying, "Oh, Griffith. Don't. Don't."[39] Then he shot her. After she had been shot, she ran toward him and scuffled with him for the gun, but while they struggled, she saw an open window and deliberately jumped from the window to get away from him. At first, Mrs. Griffith claimed Colonel Griffith was insane, but she withdrew that claim when Colonel Griffith used insanity as his defense. The jury didn't buy it. He was found guilty of assault with the intent to commit murder and sentenced to two years in San Quentin along with a $5,000 fine. Mrs. Griffith spent the rest of her life blind in her right eye as a result of the gunshot wound.

Before Griffith was a pariah, he invested money in Los Angeles real estate and purchased large tracts of land. One of the tracks he purchased was the Los Feliz Rancho, which was approximately 4,000 acres. Griffith eventually donated three-fourths of the rancho (3,015 acres) to Los Angeles for a park. He did this on December 16, 1896, and called it a "Christmas present." One of the conditions of his bequest was the city would have to improve the property for the enjoyment of its citizens. The city was slow in doing this, and Griffith must have considered taking the property back because not only was the city not improving the property but it wasn't maintaining it either. What the city was doing was leasing out some of the acreage to farmers and allowing old-growth trees to be cut down for firewood. Griffith made his disappointment known through a series of letters to the editor, and in time, the city—maybe due to shame but certainly due to the constant negative coverage in the local press—came to value the donation.

When Griffith died, his will bequeathed money for two buildings to be built in Griffith Park: the Greek Theater and Griffith Observatory.

In June 1931, the Los Angeles Parks Commission, through a resolution, approved John C. Austin and Fredric M. Ashley as the architects for the Griffith Observatory. Austin had been a major influence in the city since the erection of the Shrine Auditorium. Ashley had designed homes for the Los Angeles Investment Company and lived in Garvanza.

Griffith left $750,000 for the construction of the observatory, and the trustees of the estate were E.H. Roseberry and E.W. Widney of Security-First National Bank. While Roseberry and Widney hadn't signed off on Austin and Ashley in any legal documents, newspaper reports indicate that they did not object to the choice. Under the terms of the contract, the architects would receive a 6 percent commission on the final cost of the building. Initial press reports indicated there would be an observatory and science building. The planetarium and telescope would be constructed separately by a company called Zeiss in Jena, Germany, at costs of $75,000 and $14,600, respectively.

By October 8, 1931, Austin and Ashley had signed the contract and submitted plans, but the plans hadn't been approved by the trustees or park's commission. At a meeting held the day before, an area of contention arose: Griffith's bequest stipulated that the observatory be situated on the highest peak of Mount Hollywood, yet many park board members objected to that location. They favored a lower site, one that would be more accessible and cost less in road construction.

Six days later, the issue was put before a superior court judge Stephens. William A. Barnhill represented the trustees in the action and suggested a site west of the Greek Theater and beneath Mount Hollywood be selected instead.[40] According to Barnhill, the peak of Mount Hollywood was not an ideal location because the roads were too steep, the turns too short and the parking limited. Austin, along with Van Griffith, the donor's son, and Mabel Socha, president of the Board of Park Commissioners, all took the stand and backed Barnhill's recommendation.

On November 16, Judge Stephens announced his decision. He stated that after listening to the testimony and walking over the site, he agreed with the trustees' recommendation.[41] John Austin stated he was "gratified" by the decision and would get to work on the final drawings. The park board indicated that work on the roads to the observatory would commence immediately.

On April 23, 1933, it was announced that work would start on May 1. More details regarding the design were unveiled: the building would be two stories and two hundred feet by one hundred feet. Austin and Ashley had created a modern Greek design that would have a granite exterior (the granite was later scrapped due to safety concerns after the March 1933 Long Beach earthquake), scientific displays "both astronomical and physical" and parking for three hundred cars.

The groundbreaking took place on June 20, 1933. John Austin, who was not only one of the observatory's architects but also the chamber of commerce's chairman of the building industries committee, officiated at the ceremony. Mayor John Clinton Porter (1929–33) and Mabel Socha were two of the individuals who picked up shovels for the groundbreaking. They also spoke at the ceremony along with the head of the trustees in charge of the bequest.

On September 12, 1934, a plaster bust of Griffith Jenkins Griffith by Glendale artist Arnold Foerster was ready to be sent to the foundry. The trustees had awarded Foerster the commission, but it was Mabel Socha's idea. She felt Griffith had done a great deal for Southern California and there should be a physical reminder of him at the site.[42] (It had been thirty-two years since his trial and fifteen years since his death.) The bust was designed for a specific niche in the observatory's great hall. Foerster is also responsible for another noteworthy sculpture in Los Angeles, the Beethoven statue in Pershing Square.

On October 3, 1934, John Austin notified the Park Commission that the Simpson Construction Company had finished the observatory, although some of the painting and murals still needed to be completed. The Heisenberg Decorating Company prepared twenty sketches for the interior, and the work was approved by the board. Hugo Ballin had received the contract to paint eight murals for the ceiling and upper "celestial" areas of the walls. The murals were painted on canvas, and Ballin had delivered them, but they wouldn't be attached to the interior walls until all other painting was complete.

The planetarium shaft, or the astronomer's statue, was dedicated on November 25, 1934, and two thousand spectators showed up for the event. George Stanley, L. Archibald Garner, Arnold Foerster, Djey el Djey, Gordon Newell and Roger Burnham, the six sculptors who sculpted the shaft, were in

Griffith Observatory, unchanged since it was built. *Author photo.*

attendance and were introduced to the crowd. While Mayor Frank L. Shaw (1933–38) and Governor Frank Meriam weren't present, Mabel Socha, president of the park board, was in attendance. The artifact was described as being made of concrete, angular and bearing the likeness of six famous astronomers—Hipparchus, Copernicus, Galileo, Kepler, Newton and Herschel.[43] Two interesting points were revealed at the statue's dedication. The first was Paramount Pictures was denied permission to film parts of the building because the Zeiss contract had a provision that prevented any motion picture filming of their projector and Zeiss exercised the clause.[44] Also, the murals painted by Hugo Ballin were all copyrighted and could not be reproduced without permission.

In March 1935, two months before the observatory opened, it was reported that fencing and gates had been erected to keep the public from showing up at the site. Citizens were constantly driving up to the observatory to "look around," and they were interfering with the landscaping by trampling all over the grounds while "sight-seeing." Los Angeles was the third city in the United States, after Chicago and Philadelphia, to have a planetarium, so the *Times* wrote an article explaining its function:

> *The planetarium instrument itself is a large and complex stereopticon machine. It projects small beams of light, representing the various planets, on the inner surface of a domed ceiling and through a series of gears the rotation of the planets through their respective orbits is simulated. In the artificial heavens thus created the celestial phenomena of long periods can be observed in a short space of time and in a very impressive manner.*[45]

The dedication took place on the night of May 14, 1935, with a guest list of five hundred that included scientists, city leaders and prominent citizens. Bruce H. Grigsby, representing the trust, presented the observatory to the city. It was accepted by Mayor Shaw, who received the gift on behalf of the citizens of Los Angeles and said the observatory would always be cherished.[46] Mayor Shaw, in turn, handed custody of the observatory over to the Board of Park Commissioners. Mabel Socha accepted on behalf of the board and stated the commission would endeavor to keep the observatory always open to fulfill Colonel Griffith's dream of imparting the knowledge of the universe to the citizens of Los Angeles.

The director of the observatory, Dr. Philip Fox, provided the highlight of the evening for the invited guests gathered in the planetarium. It was reported the audience audibly gasped when the universe appeared on the ceiling of

The astronomer's statue bears the likenesses of Copernicus, Galileo and Newton along with three other astronomers. *Author photo*.

Left: John Austin, circa 1912. He had eight children, but one was his favorite. *Courtesy of* Notables of the Southwest.

Right: Meyer & Holler had offices in the Wright & Callendar Building for twenty years. John Austin, who designed the building, had an office in the building from 1910 to 1913. Elmer Grey had an office in the building from 1912 to 1916. *From the* Year Book: Los Angeles Architectural Club, *1910*.

the planetarium, and Fox supplied an extra treat by taking everyone into the future and showing how Saturn and Jupiter would be aligned in the year 1940. The Griffith Observatory opened to the public on May 15, 1935, at 10:30 a.m. The final cost of the building was approximately $500,000.[47]

Griffith Observatory was declared Los Angeles Historic Cultural Monument No. 168 on November 17, 1976.

Austin's obituary revealed that he held the No. 1 membership at the Jonathan Club, which he often mentioned with pride, and joined the club in 1903.[48] He served as president of the organization from 1916 to 1917. Austin was also a thirty-second-degree Mason. John Austin died at his home in Pasadena on September 3, 1963. He was ninety-three years old. His survivors included his third wife, Dorothy, and his seven children from his second marriage. He's buried at Mountain View Mausoleum in Altadena, California.

3
CLAUD BEELMAN

In the 1940 census, Claud Beelman stated that the highest level of education he received was the fourth year of high school, or the senior year. That's incorrect. Beelman could have been embarrassed or ashamed at his lack of education, and maybe that's why he lied to the census taker, but it could have been he was simply reinventing himself for people who knew nothing about him. Fifteen years later, in a 1955 interview with the *Lima (OH) News*, the newspaper reported, "Claud Beelman, Los Angeles, Calif., is proof that a college education isn't an essential to success in a chosen field. Nor even a high school education. He never received formal education beyond elementary level."[49] The local newspaper revealed these facts, and because they were the truth, Beelman couldn't deny them. Beelman was born on January 20, 1884, in Bellefontaine, Ohio, only thirty-five miles away from Lima, Ohio. The people of Lima and Bellefontaine would have had knowledge of Beelman's past and known Beelman had never attended high school.

Beelman's father, Daniel, was a partner in a carriage works company in Lima, where the family lived during Beelman's youth. Beelman's mother's name was Rosa, and Beelman had an older brother named William.

Once Claud began working in the architectural profession, he worked as a "cub." *Cub* was Beelman's word to describe himself and his inexperience. Beelman amusingly recalled what his apprenticeship was like: "I was very proficient in up-ending ink bottles on drawings from the very beginning, and I learned a lot from all the retracing I had to do."[50] While he spent five years working in Toledo, from 1914 to 1919, he also worked in a variety of architectural offices between the years 1900 and 1914 and in various cities, including Cleveland, Columbus, Detroit, Indianapolis, New Orleans, Philadelphia and Shreveport.

Claud Beelman, circa 1928.
Courtesy of Men of California.

During these early years, Beelman entered architectural competitions sponsored by institutions in the United States, Europe and Canada. His efforts paid off when he won a scholarship to Harvard given by the Architectural League of America in either 1905 or 1906, depending on the source. Beelman declined the scholarship, probably because he saw marriage in his future and must have pondered how he could support a wife and possibly a family as a student.

Beelman met his first wife, Lourene Taft, at a party in Spencerville, Ohio. They married in 1907 and had a daughter, Helen Louise, who was born in 1911.

After five years in Toledo, the Beelman family moved to Fort Worth; the 1920 census places them there. In 1921, the Beelman family left Omaha, Nebraska, and moved to Los Angeles.[51]

The first indication that Beelman had found employment in California was an April 2, 1922 *Los Angeles Times* article that reported Aleck Curlett and Claud Beelman as the architects for the Farmers and Merchants Bank in Long Beach, California. Beelman's partnership with Curlett would be extremely successful throughout the 1920s, and the partners would design some of the major buildings in downtown Los Angeles' historic core. One of the first buildings of note that they designed was the Pershing Square Building (1924). Located at the corner of Fifth and Hill Streets, it was a thirteen-story reinforced concrete building whose grand opening included a luncheon that Mayor George E. Cryer attended. Cryer's words at the event revolved around "the great army of workers" in Los Angeles and how modern office buildings provided "comfort" for them. In this early phase of their partnership, Curlett and Beelman entered the Arcade Building competition, which was a contest to design a height-limit building for a prime piece of Los Angeles real estate that was bound by Broadway and Spring Streets and located between Fifth

The Elks Lodge on a postcard with a view of Westlake Park in the foreground. *Author's collection.*

and Sixth Streets. They lost to Kenneth MacDonald, but Curlett and Beelman's design was featured in an article devoted to the competition's finalists in *Architect and Engineer*, and this certainly raised their profile within the state and across the nation.

ELKS LODGE

One of Curlett and Beelman's most impressive buildings was the Elks Lodge (1925), located on the southwest corner of Sixth Street and Parkview. The building is ideally situated, for not only does it overlook Westlake Park (McArthur Park), which was a desirable location when the building was erected, but it also had the added advantage of facing east, toward downtown, so the downtown skyline is visible from the building's east-facing windows.

In 1924, when the building's construction was announced, the Westlake Park area was "an exclusive residential section of the city." It was estimated that the Elks Lodge would cost $1.5 million, and the design was described as a mixture of Grecian and Syrian architecture. The Curlett and Beelman plans were approved by the Elks' building committee as of March 9, 1924.

The main building is 156 feet high, and the two wings, which are north and south, are 72 feet high. The entrance to the building is located on Parkview Street, and the lobby is 50 feet high and 25 feet wide. Newspaper accounts stated that it was Curlett and Beelman's goal to design on a large scale and overwhelm individuals who walked into the lobby.[52]

While other lodges had included commercial space on the ground floor that could be rented out for income, the Elks not only did that but, in a shrewd move, also placed 175 hotel rooms on the upper seven floors of the building with 25 rooms per floor. When built, there were single rooms and suites, all with private baths. The original configuration also contained these features: two roof gardens on the two seventy-two-foot wings. The second floor had a gymnasium and racquetball courts. A dining room, "lounging" room, ballroom and lodge room (that could seat 1,500) were all situated on the first floor. A Turkish bath, locker rooms and a "plunge"—which officially had the name of the "azure pool"—were inserted into the basement. The pool was fifty feet wide and one hundred feet long with a depth of eleven feet at its deepest point. The fourth floor contained a variety of rooms, including seven private dining rooms, a grill, a billiard room, various directors' rooms, a glee hall and a band hall.

In October 1924, the Exalted Ruler of the Elks, George M. Breslin, announced groundbreaking ceremonies for the proposed lodge. The No. 99 lodge, which was behind the building, was the largest Elks lodge in the west with 4,300 members, and the ceremony took place on a Wednesday evening at 8:30 p.m. (It was either on October 29 or November 5, but the date isn't clear in any of the reports.) The elaborate program included music provided

Left: A pair of angels from the northeast corner of the building's façade. *Right*: Above the entrance is a clock with an elk at the center of the clock's face. *Author photos*.

by the U.S. Naval Reserve Band and the Elks' band, along with speeches, tributes to past exalted leaders, the taking of photographs and the turning of the "first steam shovel full of earth." It was stressed that work on the building would continue twenty-four hours a day until it was completed.[53] According to plans, the lodge would be finished within one year. Until then, the Los Angeles Elks would continue to meet at their Angels Flight lodge at Third and Olive Streets.

The cornerstone was laid on March 28, 1925. A parade to the lodge's location, to celebrate the milestone, began at Union Avenue, between Seventh and Eighth Streets, at 1:30 p.m., and the cornerstone was scheduled to be in place by 2:30 p.m. Prominent citizen and politician Isidore B. Dockweiler was the keynote speaker at the event, but the president of the chamber of commerce and the head of the Westlake businessmen's association also addressed the crowd. Streetcar service was expected to be interrupted due to the parade.

The new lodge was completed on August 1, 1925.

The day before the lodge's official opening, in a *Times* editorial by Hiram J. Wambold, the building was viewed as "one of the showplaces of Los Angeles and a monument to man's accomplishment as a builder."[54]

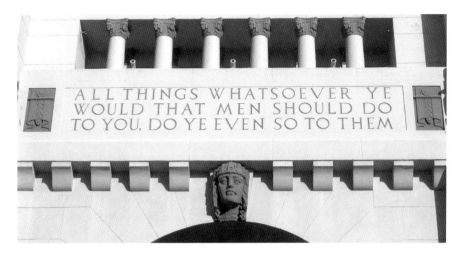

"All things whatsoever ye would that men should do to you, do ye even so to them." It is a quote from the Bible: Matthew 7:12. *Author photo*.

Relief on the façade of the Elks building. *Courtesy of Mark Snowden*.

Wambold claimed the entrance had the "grandeur of a medieval castle" and the mammoth staircase to the second floor's memorial hall was "one of the principal glories of the Elks' Temple."[55]

On May 3, 1926, the lodge finally opened. More than two thousand Elks showed up for the ceremony, which meant there wasn't enough room in the lodge room, so the overflow loitered in the lobby or on the staircase. Grand Exalted Ruler Raymond Benjamin (1914–15) accepted the hall on behalf of Lodge 99. He said, "It is an honor to participate in a ceremony of this character; commemorative of the work and progress of the order that we all love so deeply; in the dedication of a building of such beauty in the name of God and to the purposes of charity, justice and brotherly love."[56]

The building was declared Los Angeles Cultural Heritage Monument No. 267 on June 24, 1983.

Curlett and Beelman continued their charge over the Los Angeles landscape over the next few years with large impressive buildings that remain part of the downtown core. Four of them are the Barker Brothers flagship store (1926)

Close-up of metalwork that is above the entrance doors. *Author photo.*

at 818 West Seventh Street, the Chester Williams Building (1926) at 215 West Fifth Street, the Roosevelt Building (1927) at 727 West Seventh and the Foreman & Clark Building (1928) at 400 West Seventh Street. Curlett and Beelman contributed something to the downtown landscape that Thompson Mayes alluded to in his article "Why Do Old Places Matter?" What they contributed, along with the other great Los Angeles architects who designed for the historic core, is a "sense of place." Nowhere else in the Los Angeles region is there a congested and dense area where the sidewalks are crowded with people and towering buildings loom overhead. The fact that so many of these buildings survived, with much of their original detailing, is a testament to city hall, the Los Angeles Conservancy and the people of Los Angeles for valuing and wanting to preserve this important and visual part of their past.

The firm of Curlett and Beelman officially dissolved in 1932, according to the obituary of Aleck Curlett, but even before the dissolution, Beelman was designing buildings on his own. One of his first was the Garfield Building.

GARFIELD BUILDING

Garfield Building, circa 1929. A sliver of the Hill Street Theater can be seen across the street. *Courtesy of the California History Room, California State Library, Sacramento, California.*

The million-dollar, twelve-story Garfield Building (1929) was first mentioned in a newspaper account on December 16, 1928, with the headline, "Skyscraper to Rise Downtown." Construction of the building was set to begin at midnight on December 31, and it was scheduled to be completed by July 1, 1929. A mere six months.

The building is located on the northwest corner of Eighth and Hill Streets. It's Gothic in design with 58 feet of frontage on Hill Street and 160 feet of frontage on Eighth Street. Twenty-two offices grace each floor from the second to the twelfth and each floor has wainscoting in Notre Dame marble.[57] The floors in the hallways are terrazzo. Gladding-McBean supplied the terra cotta—in an off-white color—which was attached to the outside of the building.

Top: The ornate marquee of the Garfield Building. *Courtesy of the California History Room, California State Library, Sacramento, California.*

Bottom: Lobby of the Garfield Building. *Courtesy of the California History Room, California State Library, Sacramento, California.*

The marble lobby is two stories high, has three elevators and "six wall niches, framed in German silver." The center section of the building, on the Eighth Street side, is recessed from the third floor to the twelfth, which provides a light court, and "the marquee," according to architect Beelman, is "unique in its treatment of marble, nickel, illuminated glass signs and cast-iron ornament."[58]

In 1973, the Garfield Building's lobby was declared Historic Cultural Monument No. 121 by the Los Angeles Cultural Heritage Board, and on March 17, 1982, the entire building was declared a Historic Cultural Monument.

EASTERN COLUMBIA BUILDING

Construction on the Eastern Columbia Building began one minute after midnight on January 1, 1930, and the building was scheduled to be finished by July 1, 1930. While it may sound unbelievable that a thirteen-story steel and concrete building could be constructed in six months, that was the goal when construction began. On June 1, 1930, Lawrence McNeil, who was head of the company in charge of construction, the J.V. McNeil Company, stated it was possible because modern engineering methods "are in direct contrast to the now obsolete methods of a few years ago when buildings of lesser magnitude took at least a year and a half to complete."[59]

Architect Claud Beelman took a tour of eastern and midwestern department stores (Boston, Chicago, Cleveland, Detroit, New York and Philadelphia) in the summer of 1929 to study and incorporate the latest innovations into the Eastern Columbia Building. It's been widely reported over the years that one idea Beelman incorporated was to use the Eastern Columbia clock tower to house the mechanical equipment—heating, lighting and water systems—which are normally situated in the basement.

R.M. Storms was the mechanical engineer on the project. An article titled "Architecture Upside Down" stated, "Mr. Storms originated the scheme of placing the boilers next [to] the sky. He first tried out the scheme on a smaller building across Broadway, and it worked surprising well. Likewise, in this newer and greater structure, unexpected advantages have already developed."[60]

One of the advantages was that smoke from any of the mechanicals easily escaped through the clock tower's smokestack. While it cost 4 percent more to install the mechanicals on the roof, the savings in operating costs "go on forever." One of the biggest savings was space. The basement of the Eastern Columbia was used for sales instead of boilers, and according to a newspaper report from the day the store opened (it also listed the types of merchandise on each floor), the basement, or "subfloor," was used for "economy sales," likely discounted merchandise. The subfloor ended up being one of the most profitable showrooms in the building.

To support the weight of four water towers on the roof, estimated to weigh 250 tons, Storms added extra steel supports, and while this arrangement might not be advantageous for smaller buildings, Storms advocated switching mechanicals from the basement to the roof whenever possible.[61] Whoever's idea it was, Beelman's or Storms', the two agreed on the arrangement, so both men deserve credit for the innovation.

The Los Angeles–based company Gladding-McBean once again supplied the blue (aquamarine) terra-cotta tile that clads the exterior of the building. The clay products manufacturer was able to adhere gold decorative detailing to the blue tile with heat to enhance the building's streamlined modern look. According to its contract, Gladding-McBean would supply more than one thousand tons of terra cotta for the building.

The Eastern Outfitting line specialized in high-end modern furniture. The Columbia Outfitting line dealt with a variety of merchandise, including ladies' wear and accessories, men's clothing and children's apparel. For employees and customers, there was a rooftop garden, and one newspaper account stated there was a model bungalow, also on the roof, which seems appropriate for a furniture retailer. The ground floor had an L-shaped arcade and a large auditorium for employee assemblies.

The telechron electric clock has a dial on each side and uses neon for illumination. At the time of construction, there was a height limit of 150 feet for buildings in Los Angeles. The Eastern Columbia building is 235 feet tall. Beelman was able to skirt the height restriction because the 150-foot limit did not apply to the two-story penthouse that housed the mechanicals or the 50-foot clock tower that sat upon the penthouse.

The building opened on September 12, 1930, so it was nine months instead of six, but it was still considered a speed record for the construction of a height-limit building. It was also noted, at the time of its opening, that there were no serious accidents involving workmen during the building's erection.

The grand opening festivities consisted of welcoming the public from 10:00 a.m. to 10:00 p.m. but with no business being transacted.

Eastern Columbia Building at night, 1930s. *Courtesy of the California History Room, California State Library, Sacramento, California.*

The opening was a reception for the public to see the building and the merchandise available. Olive Gray, who wrote a newspaper appraisal at the time, referred to the building positively as a "stately pile of cerulean green."[62] She went onto proclaim that there are no "ugly fire ladders"[63]

Eastern Columbia Building entrance. *Courtesy of the California History Room, California State Library, Sacramento, California.*

on the outside of the building because, instead, it had "fire shafts"[64] (iron staircases) in each corner. She evaluated the ground-floor entrance as being dignified with black marble and bronze trim and succinctly summed up the building as being "in good taste without undue ostentation."[65]

According to Alan Sieroty, the grandson of the founder Adolph Sieroty, the Eastern and Columbia stores vacated the building in 1957. Sieroty went on to say, "Beelman was one of the best architects of the time and in my opinion, none of his buildings are as nice as the Eastern Columbia Building."[66]

The building was declared Los Angeles Cultural Historical Monument No. 294 on June 28, 1985.

Beelman continued to design distinctive and memorable buildings in the Los Angeles region, including the Sun Realty Building (1930) at 629 Hill Street in downtown Los Angeles, and in Hollywood, Beelman designed the Cedars of Lebanon Hospital (1930) located at 4833 Fountain Avenue, which is now used by the Church of Scientology. Beelman also designed the Hollywood Post Office (1933) at the corner of Wilcox and Selma in conjunction with Allison & Allison Architects, and by himself, Beelman designed the Metro-Goldwyn-Mayer Administrative Building (1938) in Culver City.

In his personal life, after his first wife died in 1948, Beelman remarried in 1949. His second wife's name was Ann.

Beelman said the secret to his success was "hard work and close attention to all details."[67] He got his greatest satisfaction, architecturally, from "solving the problems of each new project and following its evolution from the idea stage to the finished structure."[68]

Claud Beelman died on January 30, 1963. His death was attributed to injuries he received in a 1961 automobile accident. He had been living in Laguna Beach at the time of his death and was buried at Forest Lawn's Church of the Recessional. His survivors include his wife, Ann; daughter, Helen Marley; and grandson, Lawrence Marley. His obituary revealed one final interesting fact. It stated Beelman designed "the familiar Dutch windmill for Van de Kamp bakeries."[69]

4
ELMER GREY

E lmer Grey could have had a much bigger career, but he decided that wasn't what he wanted because he knew it wouldn't make him happy. Some of the buildings Grey is associated with are the Wattles Mansion (1908) at 1824 North Curson Avenue, which is now owned by the City of Los Angeles; the Huntington home (1911) located in San Marino, California, and part of the Huntington Museum complex; and the Lincoln Shrine (1932) in Redlands, California.

Elmer Grey was born on April 29, 1872, in Chicago. He was the son of Henry C. Grey and Caroline (née Johns). Grey went to public schools in Milwaukee but received no formal architectural training at either a university or college. He received his only architectural training by working, for three years, as a draftsman in the Milwaukee architectural office of Ferry and Clas.

Grey opened an architectural office in Milwaukee in 1900, when he was twenty-eight. Over thirty years later, he wrote about his early practice in a nine-part series called "Vicissitudes of a Young Architect" for the publication *Architect and Engineer*. In it, he bluntly states that he found striking out on his own "terrifying." He had given up a regular paycheck working for an architectural firm, but it wasn't by choice. He was forced to leave but didn't elaborate as to the reason.

"Mental strain" or "nervous tension" would likely have been the most obvious reasons for his departure.

Grey set up an office on the third floor in the same building as his former employer. He did this because he hoped to pick up surplus work from the firm if no work of his own materialized.

Prior to being "let go," Grey had designed and built a bachelor cottage, for his own use, at Fox Pointe, which was a new resort on the outskirts of Milwaukee. Grey, looking back, thought he was foolish to have built it because he didn't need it, but his foolishness paid off. The location, he claimed, made it noteworthy. Sitting on a bluff that overlooked Lake Michigan, the building gained attention as the resort became more fashionable. Not only was it eventually featured in an architectural magazine but it was used in a building advertisement as well, which seemed to elicit some amusement in Grey when he recounted the advertisement. Grey claimed his bachelor's folly brought him to the attention of the American Institute of Architects and it gave him entree to that organization.

Best of all, he gained clients due to the cottage's prominence. He was making more money than he had previously, receiving larger commissions and "headed under full steam toward a brilliant and successful future,"[70] but it didn't happen. Not right away. He claimed what occurred was due to strenuous exercise and too much "mental work."[71] Then he wrote that "slowly but surely"[72] his health was undercut. He had just finished plans for a Christian Science church "when my health broke down completely."[73] He stated that his clients tried to help him through his crisis, but their concern wasn't enough.

Whatever was troubling Grey, he fled from it. He moved to Florida and never returned to his Milwaukee office on the third floor. After attempting to recuperate in Florida, Grey traveled to Philadelphia to consult with the prominent nerve specialist Dr. S. Weir Mitchell. Mitchell promoted a "rest cure" for men and women who had neurasthenia, which was considered a nervous disorder due to too much stress from living in a fast-paced, modern world. Mitchell's advice to Grey was pretty standard. He advised him to go out west and work on a ranch away from the pressures of urban living.

Grey ended up on a dude ranch in Las Vegas that Mitchell had recommended, but he didn't like it. It was, Grey said, "a boarding house situated in the midst of an uninteresting expanse of barren country with a goodly sum charged for the use of a horse."[74] When the opportunity to escape to California arose, he grabbed it and ended up living on Catalina Island. For four months, he played tennis, fished, swam and sailed in a tiny craft he purchased. According to the *Pasadena Star News*, Grey "built up his strength forfeited through his nervous breakdown."[75] Yet all the rest made him restless. When he saw an advertisement in the newspaper for a ranch hand in Hollywood that paid twenty-five dollars a month and included board, he applied for the job and was hired.

The ranch was situated in the center of Hollywood and consisted of nine acres of orange trees. There was a house, a barn and a small irrigating reservoir that Grey would eventually use for bathing. Grey wrote in "Vicissitudes," "Where then were unpaved country lanes overarched with drooping pepper trees, tall office buildings now rise. Where then were dimly lighted streets, Neon signs now blaze forth at night and Klieg lights shoot fingers of light into the sky announcing film premiers."[76]

The Hollywood Hotel, which opened in 1902, was the place Grey went for his Sunday dinner and to socialize in the evenings. He stated that he was the subject of much gossip because he was a ranch hand and many of the guests did not see him as their equal. Some wouldn't even talk to him. Grey commented that he was "a stable boy by day and a socialite by night."[77] One person who valued his worth was the proprietress of the hotel. Wrote Grey, "When I resumed my architectural practice some years later the manager of the Hollywood Hotel became the leading spirit in the project of building the Beverly Hills Hotel, a $200,000 enterprise, and to him who she had formerly known as a ranch hand she gave the commission of planning it!"[78]

Before the Beverly Hills Hotel project, Grey entered into a partnership with Myron Hunt, whom he met while horseback riding near Monrovia, California. In an installment of "Vicissitudes of a Young Architect," Grey recalls how they formed their firm, which existed from 1904 to 1910, but his health failed again during their collaboration. He wrote, "In my partnership with Mr. Hunt the arrangement, at first, was that I should spend only a short time each day in the office until my nerves got in better shape."[79] During their partnership, they designed numerous projects, including the main building for Pasadena's California Institute of Technology. In this decade, Grey was also appointed to the art committee of the St. Louis World's Fair (1904) but was unable to serve.[80] On January 27, 1906, he married Millicent Bowers in Pasadena, California.

BEVERLY HILLS HOTEL

Margaret J. Anderson, the woman who had been running the Hollywood Hotel since 1901, was the person responsible for the creation of the Beverly

Hills Hotel, which opened in 1912. Anderson obtained the land herself from the Percy H. Clark Company in 1911, and from the start, she envisioned the Beverly Hills Hotel as a hotel that would cater to the "highest class tourist and family patronage."[81]

She selected Elmer Grey as the architect, and when the construction of the hotel was announced, the announcement included notification that Grey would also design a number of lavish homes for the immediate surrounding area, which would be "the showplaces of the southland."[82] The homes were slated to go up concurrently with the hotel.

Originally, the hotel would have three hundred rooms, and the initial cost of construction, in May 1911, was estimated to be $500,000. Four months later, in September 1911, the cost was lowered and broken down as follows: $200,000 for the hotel, $45,000 for furnishings, $35,000 for landscaping and $20,000 for a reinforced automobile garage.

The building would be in the California Mission style. In the architectural renderings of Elmer Grey's design, a long, porch would grace the length of the hotel and be one of the key elements that welcomed visitors, along with the three mission towers. Grey's porch treatment was handled differently, for it was not covered as was usual in Mission-style architecture. Instead, in a nod to California and its abundant sunshine, in place of a roof was a long pergola that permitted light to cascade down through slats, illuminating the sidewalk below and the rooms that fronted the porch. According to the touted plans, a pergola theme would permeate the hotel's exterior and create an indoor-outdoor living arrangement. The front of the hotel would be

Early image of the Beverly Hills Hotel while still under construction. *From the* Year Book: Los Angeles Architectural Club, *1912.*

Beverly Hills Hotel in a view looking north. *Courtesy of the California History Room, California State Library, Sacramento, California.*

Beverly Hills Hotel, circa 1913. *Courtesy of the California History Room, California State Library, Sacramento, California.*

parallel to Sunset Boulevard, and because it sat on a large knoll, it offered not only ocean and mountain views but also vistas of Hollywood and way off in the distance, downtown Los Angeles.

The hotel's original shape was in the form of a letter *T*. Private baths would be standard in most rooms along with telephone service and steam heat. Eighteen rooms would have personal verandahs that could be used as sleeping porches, and fourteen rooms would have balconies. Private dining rooms were planned for the hotel, and the main dining room was designed to handle five hundred hotel guests at any time. While no swimming pool was mentioned, the hotel's amenities included tennis courts, a playground, a livery stable, a garage, a drugstore, a post office, a library and a barbershop.

The Alta Planing Mill Company was given the contract for the construction of the building. Stanley Anderson, Margaret's son, would manage the hotel. It was slated to open April 1, 1912, and while the opening date was eventually moved to May 1, the delay did not deter guests. On the day the hotel opened, all three hundred rooms were booked.

FIRST CHURCH OF CHRIST, SCIENTIST

During the 1910s, Grey worked for the Christian Science society and had input into the types of buildings the society built. In Los Angeles, Grey designed the First Church of Christ, Scientist (1914).

Elmer Grey wrote in an article for *Architectural Record*,

> *It should be an axiom that religious organizations should always build well. The commercial spirit of our age is so inclined to be a mad race for the "almighty dollar," and commercial structures are so often built with the idea of obtaining the most show for the least money that when religious organizations build they should show that their aims are higher. The trend of preachment or sermons in all churches is for the things of lasting value, the real as against the seeming; so when a church builds, it should show that it believes in putting such preachments into practice, that it demands the real in architecture instead of that which only seems so. Many people of taste and discrimination will judge it thus, by its acts rather than by its words.*[83]

Plans for the church were announced on September 19, 1911. Few details were released, but it was noted the church would be located at the corner of Alvarado and Alvarado Terrace, Elmer Grey was selected as the architect and the cost was estimated to be $100,000. More details surfaced over the following months, among them: the church would be Italian Romanesque in style and occupy the entire lot, which was diamond shaped and approximately 178 by 144 feet. There would be seating for 1,050 in the main auditorium and seating for 250 in the balcony.

The building was designed to be of reinforced concrete up to the first-floor level and have exterior walls of brick with tapestry brick facing, a clay tile roof and leaded glass windows.

Grey wrote that an important issue with designing a church for a new denomination was what it needed was different from what other churches have needed in the past

> *because excellence in architecture, as in other things, comes from a gradual process of development, from an improvement of good things already done rather than from a sudden bursting forth of some fine new thing. The church architecture of the remote past, by such a process of development and adaptation to the varying conditions of different countries finally culminated in the splendid Gothic, Romanesque and Renaissance cathedrals of England, France and Italy; and these wonderful monuments have in their turn provided the inspiration for most of the best church architecture of the present day.*

Yet his quote could also be seen as advocating for the use of historic idioms in church architecture.

For this church, a large foyer where the congregation could meet and talk after the service was requested. The building committee also stated since the congregation wanted to view the rostrum and hear the sermon they didn't want a long auditorium, which is often found in churches, but instead a broad room. Grey advocated for listening to clients and stated, "Such departures should be made unhesitatingly."[84]

Sketches of the church were displayed at the third exhibition of the Los Angeles Architectural Club, held from February 23 to March 15, 1912. According to the *Christian Science Sentinel*, "Four services were not sufficient to accommodate all who wished to attend the formal opening of the new First Church of Christ, Scientist, Alvarado and Hoover Streets, Sunday (January 4, 1914). There must be an extraordinary power in a movement that is not sensational, sentimental, sensuous or striking in any of its doctrines or observances."[85] Since Christian Science churches aren't dedicated until

First Church of Christ, Scientist. *Author photo.*

they are debt free, the church was not dedicated until Sunday, November 25, 1918. The church was later sold and, at one time, used by Jim Jones's Peoples Temple. It is presently a Seventh-day Adventist church.

The church was declared Los Angeles Historic Cultural Monument No. 89 on July 7, 1971.

Few details are available concerning Millicent's death, but Grey's first wife died on October 20, 1915. Two years later, the *Los Angeles Herald* printed a brief wedding announcement regarding Grey's second marriage to Anabel Rohrbacher. Their marriage took place in the garden of Grey's home on April 18, 1917, and Grey's daughter from his first marriage, Virginia, was the flower girl. The new couple honeymooned in Riverside, California, and then returned to Pasadena to live in the home Grey designed. Because of the First World War, Grey turned to the motion picture industry for a few years and soon was on the staff of Columbia Studios, where he planned new buildings, numerous sets and fireproof film vaults.[86] He also continued to design private homes during the 1910s and had no major commissions until he designed the Pasadena Playhouse, which opened in 1925.

PASADENA PLAYHOUSE

In 1917, Gilmore Brown organized the Pasadena Community Playhouse Association, and that act, on his part, resulted in what is known today as the Pasadena Playhouse. In the initial years, the Playhouse group met and performed in an old burlesque theater on South Fair Oaks, and one of the players' inspirations was to carry out the strong edict of writer and dramatist Percy MacKaye, who was against the commercial theater and the moneymaking aspect of it. In his 1909 book *The Playhouse and the Play*, MacKaye examined the role of the theater in the community and asked if the playhouse's function is "to produce civic-inspiring art," how can the playhouse be "left to perform its proper function, utterly exposed to the temptations and corruptions of commercial supply and demand?"[87]

In the first year, while the principal roles played in Playhouse productions were paid and performed by professional actors, the smaller roles were unpaid and performed by amateurs. This formula created friction among the actors, so in the second year, a different approach was taken: all the roles and all the functions related to the Playhouse—acting, costumes, lighting, scenery and directing—were performed voluntarily. As the Playhouse's membership and support increased over the next seven years, there came a point where a more permanent theater building was needed, and in February 1924, the Pasadena Community Guild Organization was formed for the specific purpose of "erecting a new building for the community Playhouse."[88] It was stated at this time that "the Pasadena Community Playhouse is perhaps the most unique civic organization to be found in the United States. It is a nonprofit organization made up of prominent Pasadena people who are interested, for the sake of art alone."[89]

Construction began on May 12, 1924, and was expected to be finished by April 1, 1925. The estimated cost of the building varied in news reports between $200,000 and $250,000. Outright donations accounted for 75 percent of the money raised at this juncture, and stock was sold as a funding source too. Elmer Grey was selected as the architect, and the Playhouse was designed to seat 800 people, though the final seat count was 820.

An update on the progress of the theater in September 1924 mentioned that the cornerstone had been laid in June during the Drama League of America convention, which was held in Pasadena, and the Winter Construction Company had the contract for the building's construction. Pasadena, which was originally referred to as the Indiana Colony—individuals from the state of Indiana bought large tracts in the community—became known in the early twentieth century as the Crown City. According to newspaper reports, the Pasadena Community Playhouse "promises to be one of the show-places of the Crown City."[90]

Pasadena Playhouse courtyard, 1920s. *Courtesy of the California History Room, California State Library, Sacramento, California.*

The Playhouse was scheduled to open on May 18, 1925, and the papers could hardly contain their excitement. In one newspaper article alone were these two sentences: "Opening night is expected to be the greatest social function of the year in this city" and "All Pasadena aristocracy will be present for the colorful affair."[91] The cast for the opening night production of *Amethyst* by Victor Mapes was not revealed in advance but included a variety of talent ranging from local college students and professors to a rich and well-known lawyer, a salesman, a grocer and "several society women from the most exclusive Pasadena circles."[92]

The opening was the fulfillment of a dream for many citizens in the Crown City who worked together for a common goal, and the Playhouse was a visible display of the will of the community. One reporter noted, "This is what a non-profit organization, an organization untinged by the touch of commercialism, can do."[93] As for the building, some referred to it as "Early Californian," better known today as Mission Revival architecture. Patrons of the Playhouse were greeted by a small, square patio enclosed on three sides; the fourth side opened to the street. An *L*-shaped arched colonnade ran along the north and west sides of the patio overlooked by a trio of palm trees. The building itself was constructed of reinforced concrete, and the interior was designed in the Spanish Renaissance style by A. Dwight Gibbs.

The original green room situated under the stage had dressing rooms, makeup rooms, lockers, showers and a kitchen. It was advertised as the place where the cast and the audience could meet and mingle after the show.

Opening night included musicians in Spanish garb playing guitars in the courtyard. *Times* newspaperman Edwin Schallert, who reviewed the evening, wrote the event had "the glamour of a premier."[94]

The Pasadena Playhouse is listed in the National Register of Historic Places.

In the last "Vicissitudes" installment, Elmer Grey wrote mainly about mental health. Said Grey:

- "...our mental processes play a far more important part in determining our physical welfare that hitherto has been supposed."
- "Those who are especially proficient at tasks requiring creative imagination are apt to be more sensitive than others and consequently more easily thrown off their mental balance— which in its turn effects their physical balance."

Above: Pasadena Playhouse proscenium and stage. *Courtesy of the California History Room, California State Library, Sacramento, California.*

Right: Architect Elmer Grey, circa 1932. *Courtesy of* Architect and Engineer.

- "I am convinced that many sensitive young architects have been stricken with illness at times, simply because their mental makeups go awry under that kind of strain and their physical machinery is thrown out of order in consequence."[95]

Near the very end, Grey notes that "there may be some who would say that I am not competent to give advice on the subject of professional success; that the limited nature of my architectural practice does not warrant it."[96] He countered this line of thought by asserting, rightly, that not everyone wants the same kind of success—success can't be measured by a big bank account. What's more, he had no desire for the stress of a large office, numerous employees, quick lunches and the constant ringing of a phone. Grey stated that he liked going home at a certain time every day and enjoyed the "hands on" process of creating sketches and drawings himself.

He finished the series by revealing at what stage he received the most enjoyment from his work as an architect:

> *Many people suppose that an architect's pleasure in his work is in direct proportion to the number of commissions he receives; and because, they reason, each piece of work is, when finished, a monument upon which he may look as his own. Not to any great extent is that true. The joy of all kinds of artistic work does not lie principally in the finished product, but chiefly in the creative process. That which furnishes the chief delight is the wonderful thrill one feels when the creative impulse is at the full surge of its flow. By the time a building is completed this impulse has spent itself, vexations of construction may have intervened and the pleasure in the result is largely confined to the public.*[97]

Grey died in 1963 at the age of ninety-two in the home he designed for himself at 1372 South El Molino in Pasadena. His survivors included his wife, Anabel Hubbard; a daughter, Mrs. Charles Forrester of Milwaukee; and a stepdaughter, Mrs. J.L. Cotton of Pasadena.

5
HUDSON & MUNSELL

I n 1905, architect Frank D. Hudson was in court for "driving an automobile at a speed greater than twelve miles an hour." Two officers with the last names of Allen and Majonier used stopwatches to calculate Hudson's speed and testified in court that Hudson was going "faster than twenty miles an hour." Hudson, who was the former building superintendent of Los Angeles, hired former city council member Bob Todd to defend him in the case. A fine of fifty dollars was the penalty Hudson faced if found guilty.

Hudson had two lines of defense. The first was "he had not used the special speed gear on his machine and could not have gone faster than ten or twelve miles an hour." The second was a witness. The witness was an architect friend, who was not named in the newspaper article, but claimed he was extremely nervous in automobiles and told Hudson he would not get in the car unless Hudson drove slowly. This unnamed architectural witness stated in court, "I didn't want to rush along like a cloud in a gale and the speed at which Hudson was running was perfectly satisfactory to me." Hudson's witness also testified, "Hudson had not used the rapid gear!"[98] The judge ruled in Hudson's favor despite both officers' testimony, and Hudson was ecstatic with his victory.

Frank D. Hudson was born to Henry S. Hudson and Mary (née Muir) Hudson in Oakland, California, on January 31, 1868. Until 1879, he attended public schools in California and then from 1879–85 attended the London International College in London, England. He worked for the San Francisco architect William Curlett from 1885 to 1895 but moved to Los

Architect Frank D. Hudson, circa 1920. *Courtesy of the Seaver Center for Western History Research, Los Angeles County Museum of Natural History.*

Angeles in 1887 and established his own architectural practice in 1895. For two years, starting in 1899, he was the building superintendent for the City of Los Angeles. Mayor Fred Eaton (1898–1900) appointed him to this position. He married Harriet L. Beebe on September 30, 1890, and they had a daughter named Doris in 1893.

Hudson formed a partnership with W.A.O. Munsell in October 1901, and in 1902, the firm was involved with the planning of the new Los Angeles County Jail. Some jail builders, who wanted a crack at the job, leveled charges that Hudson's drawings and specifications favored the John Pauley Jail Company in St. Louis. Hudson responded rather forcefully:

I have endeavored to favor no one; we have striven to invite competition from everywhere and shut out none. Yet before this board, insinuations have been cast that I have tried to be partial. I want to deny it. Investigate these specifications thoroughly and if it is found that, I have lied to you Supervisors in saying that all builders can bid on them equally, knock them out and draw up new ones. Since last week, a party brought me a message from a purported friend, urging me to be careful for my own good about these jail specifications and be fair. Well, gentlemen, I want to say now to whoever sent me that warning, let him talk to me personally. I don't care who he is. I am old enough to take care of myself.[99]

Hudson was upset because he felt the innuendo made him appear dishonest. The jail was eventually finished, and city officials thought well enough of Hudson to award him a contract for an additional ward to house the insane in 1904. During these early years of their partnership, Hudson & Munsell designed single-family bungalows, a three-story hotel in San Pedro, the Southern California Music Company Building on Broadway and a two-story apartment house on Hill Street. Hudson & Munsell also teamed up with John C. Austin in 1902 and submitted plans for the Pasadena City Hall competition, but they lost and had to be content with a second-place finish. In 1905, Hudson & Munsell were

The Hudson & Munsell Shrine Auditorium. It burned to the ground in 1920. *Author's collection.*

in the process of constructing the largest Scottish Rite Cathedral in the world on Hope Street between Ninth and Tenth Streets in Los Angeles. The building has been demolished, but it was "a classic structure of brick and terra cotta, in Ionic style of architecture, the technical plans for which were drawn by Architects Hudson & Munsell on lines suggested mainly by Perry W. Weldner, president of the Masonic building committee."[100] Hudson & Munsell also designed the original Shrine Auditorium, at the corner of Jefferson and Royal Streets, that burned down in 1920. This is according to a *Los Angeles Herald* article stating *that* Shrine auditorium was scheduled to have a "seating capacity for 5,000" and "the exterior will be of Mooresque design and highly ornamented."[101]

Another substantial commission came to Hudson & Munsell in 1906.

THE MASONIC TEMPLE

A newspaper article on December 28, 1906, reported the Masons had acquired a property on the southwest corner of Figueroa and Pico Streets to erect a new temple. Adelle Lauth sold the property to the Masons for the sum of $100,000.

The old temple, which was built a decade earlier for $50,000 on South Hill Street, was sold to the Los Angeles Pacific Company, which planned to demolish the building and use the location for "their great electric railway station."[102] When the Masons erected this Hill Street lodge, many individuals, Masons included, felt the lodge was too far south and away from the city's center, almost suburban. With the city's growth, the Masons were proven right to have built so far south. When the Los Angeles Pacific Company paid the organization $185,000 for the property, the Masons made a profit too. One condition of the sale was the Masons had to be out of their building by December 1907, which gave them one year to erect a new lodge building.

Preliminary plans called for a three-story lodge building with first-floor commercial stores on both Pico and Figueroa that the Masons planned to rent out for income. The second and third floors would be devoted to "modern" lodge and assembly rooms. The estimated cost was $150,000.

Over five thousand lodge members would use the new lodge, including various chapters of the Eastern Star, the Knights Templar, the Blue Lodges of Southern California and the Royal Arch Masons.

An update on the building's progress in January 1907 indicated the architects chosen for the building were Hudson & Munsell, and once the home on the property was sold and moved, construction would begin.

By September 1907, the foundation had been completed and some of the steel skeleton erected. While the building was only three stories high, it appeared to be much larger because the lodge rooms were twenty-two feet in height.

Plans indicated the main entrance, which would include a tile floor and marble stairs, would be on Pico Street, and access to the upper floors would be via an electric elevator. The first floor would have two blue lodge rooms (both forty by sixty feet) separated by a banquet room (twenty by sixty feet). On the second floor would be the Eastern Star headquarters, a Masonic library and various directors' rooms. The third floor would include an asylum for the commandery, a chapter room, a Blue Lodge room, lockers, an organ loft and banquet room. A revised estimated cost for the building, located at 1301 to 1305 South Figueroa, was $106,701.

The temple's dedication took place on November 21, 1908, almost a year later than expected. Grand Master of the State of California Oscar Lawler oversaw the ceremony:

> *The dedicatory service was then conducted according to the customs that have come down through the centuries since the dedication by King Solomon of his great temple at which all Masonry originated. Corn, oil and wine were poured upon the emblem of the lodge in compliance with the ancient rites, and after each section of the service, music floated downward from a hidden balcony.*[103]

After the dedication, the building was "open for inspection and a pageant of beautiful women wandered through, prying as far as possible into the mysterious secrets of the place. There were plenty of Masons in attendance who explained everything about the lodge rooms, except the very things that their fair companions desired to know most."[104]

The night's festivities also included a reception for Lawler, refreshments in the banquet rooms and dancing. The *Times* deemed it a "magnificent spectacle witnessed by 1,200 Masons and their ladies." The Los Angeles convention center now occupies the site where the Masonic Temple stood.

William A.O. Munsell first appeared in a Los Angeles city directory in 1897 as part of the firm Locke & Munsell with offices in the Bradbury Block and a residence on the northwest corner of Adrian and Hedding Streets. In

The Masonic Temple at Pico and Figueroa, circa 1908. *Courtesy of* Architect and Engineer.

1898, Munsell moved to the Garvanza neighborhood in Los Angeles, which was a rustic area north of the city.

In August 1901, a newspaper report announced that the partnership of Seymour E. Locke and W.A.O. Munsell had dissolved by mutual consent, but both would be staying together, for the time being, in their offices in the Potomac Block. Two months later, Munsell formed a partnership with Frank D. Hudson, so maybe Munsell was planning to team up with Hudson when he broke up with Locke.

William A.O. Munsell was born on March 2, 1866. His father was Elmore Munsell, and his mother's name was Emily. Munsell was born in Coldwater, Ohio, and had three sisters, Allie, Ladessa and Blanche.

Munsell's first wife, Octavia S. Winder, whom he married on June 25, 1891, died in 1902 according to a *Times* article headlined "Death of Mrs. Munsell." The article stated, "News comes from Portland, Or., of the death of Mrs. Octavia S. Munsell in that city on the 1st inst. Deceased was the wife of W.A.O. Munsell, the well-known architect of this city and had a wide circle of friends." Munsell had two daughters, Helen and Elizabeth, with his first wife. By 1910, Munsell had remarried. His second wife's name was Julia Van Dine, and she was born in Wisconsin. The family of four lived on Lumber Avenue in a house they owned in San Gabriel Township. According to the 1910 census, William A.O. Munsell and Julia Van Dine had been married for eighteen years, but that can't be right (he couldn't be married to two women at the same time), so the census taker must have made a mistake.

While Hudson & Munsell were working on the Masonic Temple, they received one of the biggest commissions of their careers.

LOS ANGELES COUNTY HALL OF RECORDS

The Los Angeles County Board of Supervisors took its initial step toward safeguarding the city's records in December 1907 by authorizing Hudson & Munsell to make a "preliminary sketch" for the proposed annex to the courthouse. The land needed for the annex was directly south of the courthouse and bounded by Temple, Broadway and New High (Spring) Streets. The *old* county jail and the courthouse's heating plant stood on the site along with various commercial buildings that the city did not own.

Acquiring the land, through either eminent domain or outright purchase, was the dilemma the supervisors had to confront, and the cost of the land necessary for the project had doubled in the years since the board first considered building a new hall of records.

Money for the land acquisition and the building's foundation was provided by a tax levy, which was expected to raise $300,000 and be used for the initial costs of the project. At this early date, it was not clear how many stories would be built, but the foundation would be designed to support ten stories.

The board of supervisor's chairman, Charles E. Patterson, said,

> *It may not be necessary just now to build to that height. We can put up five or six stories or as many as may be needed for our present wants but we should look forward fifteen or twenty years and make it possible in the future to add to the height. If the present courthouse had been provided with a suitable foundation, or if the walls had been made sufficiently thick we could have put on another story or two.*[105]

Three months later, in March 1908, a newspaper article had more details. The Hall of Records, seen in a Hudson & Munsell drawing, was proclaimed a fit companion to the county courthouse, and condemnation proceedings began for acquiring the land and buildings that occupied the site.

E.H. Winas, who owned some of the land the county wanted to acquire along with a building that stood upon it, was eager to sell. He wanted $60,000 for the land and $16,000 for the building, and the board members found this to be a reasonable asking price. Winas described his predicament:

> *For five years the county has been planning to build on this piece of land with the result that there has been so much uncertainty as to when it would begin condemnation proceedings that it has materially hurt any disposition I might have made of this building and land. It has also hurt my renting of the place to tenants because I could never tell when they would be forced to move out to make way for the county. It is time that this uncertainty was ended.*[106]

Frank D. Hudson said of the proposed building plans, "We have made no attempt to match the architecture of the old courthouse. What we have sought is to design a practical building which will fulfill the needs of the county for offices and make of it a modern office building with added facilities for the tremendous amount of work which has to be accomplished."[107]

Departments would not wait until the building was finished before moving in, but rather the move-in date for the various departments would commence once the first five floors were finished. On the first floor, the entire twenty-two thousand square feet would be devoted to the recorder's office, and special steel cases were purchased to protect the city's historical records from fire. The second floor was allocated to the city auditor and treasurer on the Broadway side with each taking a wing. The board of supervisors would have offices on the High Street side. On the third floor, the assessor would be on the Broadway side, and the tax collector would have both wings on High Street. On the fourth floor, both Broadway wings would be devoted to the law library, while the surveyor and the school superintendent's office would each have a wing on High Street. The sixth floor would be devoted to county township offices and courtrooms along with their officials and clerks.

Ten months later, the plans and specifications for the Hall of Records were completed and submitted to the board of supervisors for approval. They were approved. The old county jail (which was sometimes referred to as the "detention home") and the building adjacent to it had not been demolished yet, but an advertisement for bids had been placed. It was anticipated ground would be broken for the Hall of Records by March 1909.

Almost two years later, in January 1911, rumors circulated at city hall and the courthouse that men were being discouraged from working on the Hall of Records and that only 15 men were presently at work on the building. These rumors could have been started by local union leaders who were unhappy that this was a non-union job. Supervisor Sidney Allcutt Butler, chairman of the housing committee, took it upon himself to find out the truth and reported to the board of supervisors that 164 men, from electricians to structural ironworkers, were currently engaged in the completion of the project.

A month later, an article attempted to capsulize what had occurred up to that point:

- Local union officials and workers referred to the building as the Big White Building.
- It was anticipated the building would be completed by July 1, 1911.
- The final cost was estimated to be $1,025,000.
- The third floor was scheduled to be completed before any other floor and occupied by the assessor and the tax collector.
- The building would save the county $10,000 a month in rent payments to house various departments around the city, though other sources reported this amount to be $25,000.
- The Hall of Records was built to relieve congestion.
- The recorder's workers would have a special lunchroom with adjoining restrooms and available telephones where they could make private phone calls.
- There would be large interior light wells to make every office an outside office.
- Carl Leonardt was the contractor.
- Llewellyn Iron Works was in charge of the structural iron.

This newspaper account also detailed the friction between the contractor and the men working on the building. What caused the animosity occurred when land was being excavated for the Hall of Records' foundation and "large qualities of dirt close to the courthouse caved in."[108] Many connected with the project felt the courthouse was in danger of potential collapse, so the board of supervisors authorized the contractor "to work his men extra hours under an emergency clause of the laws regulating labor."[109]

Union leaders objected to the Hall of Records workers working extra hours, and although this was not a union job, union leaders contacted an

Aerial view of the Hall of Records. *Courtesy of the California History Room, California State Library, Sacramento, California.*

attorney and tried to have the Hall of Records' contractor, Carl Leonardt, fined. The board of supervisors upheld Leonardt's action, which caused the ironworkers to join the union and immediately go on strike. The clue that the ironworkers were on strike was no one at the courthouse could hear the sound of riveting anymore. It suddenly became completely silent. The board of supervisors chose to end the strike by hiring "free men" who were non-union workers. This is interesting and important for a variety of reasons but mainly because on September 10, 1910, union workers attempted to dynamite the Hall of Records. According to court testimony in the months that followed, it was revealed that on the morning of September 10, 1910, just before 1:00 a.m., police officers went to the Hall of Records because of a phone tip received that was put into court records as, "There is a determined plot to blow up the Hall of Records at 1 o'clock this morning. You'd better get busy, and quick too."[110]

Since dynamite had been found at the Alexandria Annex, which was under construction at the time, police officers took the phone call seriously. When they arrived, they found nothing out of the ordinary and no signs of an explosion, but an officer named Abel was patrolling the worksite when he bumped into a man in the darkness. Patrolman Abel said, "Why don't you look where you're going?"[111] The only response Abel received was a punch on the chin, and then his assailant fled on foot. The patrolman was "taken back" but regained his bearings, pursued the man and, when his attacker tripped and fell near Broadway, captured him. The assailant was Bert H. Connors—a union man.

What followed was a long court trial that ended in a "hung jury," but

Entrance to the Hall of Records. *Courtesy of the California History Room, California State Library, Sacramento, California.*

Connors and his codefendants, A.B. Maple and F. Ira Pender, were badgered by the legal system for various infractions for years to come. It appears as if lawyers working for the city and the county figured if they couldn't "get them" for one thing they would "get them" for something else.

The opening of the Hall of Records and the subsequent moving in of the departments became secondary to the court proceedings that occurred as the building was being finished. The completion of the building paled in comparison with headlines that included: "Crowds Storm Court House Like Wolves" and "Labor Temple Net of Unionite Dynamiters." There was some criticism concerning the delays in the opening of the building and a few lawsuits were filed over payments and work not being up to specifications, but eventually all the departments moved into the building. The Hall of Records stood as a monument to both Los Angeles' desire to safeguard its recorded history and to the architectural firm of Hudson & Munsell until the building was demolished in 1973.

NATURAL HISTORY MUSEUM OF LOS ANGELES COUNTY

The city, county and state were all involved in the construction of the Natural History Museum, which was originally called the Museum of Art, Science and History. When the building was conceived by Hudson & Munsell, it was designed in the form of a cross with three distinct wings. The west wing would be the historical museum. The east wing would house the natural science collection, and the south wing would be two stories high and house an art gallery.

But it wasn't only the Museum of Art, Science and History that was planned for the site, which was then called Agricultural Park. Also included in the concept were an armory building and an exposition building being designed by the state architect W.D. Coates Jr. and state engineer N. Emery, respectively. The cost budgeted for each building was as follows: armory, $100,000; Museum of Art, Science and History, $150,000; exposition building, $250,000. The City of Los Angeles also committed $100,000 to landscape the park, and the original plan called for rockeries, lily ponds, landscaped lawns, sunken gardens and fruit trees. There was a playground planned for the northwest corner and an Owens River Memorial Fountain, which was to cost $75,000 and adorn one of the entrances.

The Museum of Art, Science and History was designed to be a formal building in the Spanish Renaissance style with a dome eighty feet in diameter. The rotunda, which would sit under the interior's stained-glass dome, would have a diameter of seventy feet with a balcony that encircled it and be supported by sixteen scagliola marble columns. Bathrooms, storage areas and workrooms were planned for the basement.

The building would be constructed of reinforced concrete and have a red tapestry brick exterior and red tile roof. Its length, across the front, would be 310 feet, and the depth to the end of the art gallery would be 176 feet.

Four months later, in April 1910, three important developments occurred. First, state architect W.D. Coates Jr. had brought state-approved plans to Los Angeles, and second, state engineer N. Emery was accepting bids from contractors for construction of the museum. The third was an announcement that an agreement had been reached and signed between the City of Los Angeles and four groups to curate the Museum of Art, Science and History. The four groups were the Historical Society of Southern California, the Fine Arts League, the Southern California Academy of Science and the Cooper Ornithological Club (southern division). A nine-person committee representing the four groups was established, and two members of note on that committee were George Finley Bovard, president of USC, and William M. Bowen, whom everyone referred to as the "father of Agricultural Park."[112] Bowen was repeatedly mentioned in newspaper accounts as being instrumental in doing the groundwork that persuaded state officials to take over Agricultural Park on "behalf of the state of California."[113]

A groundbreaking ceremony for the new park, overseen by Lieutenant Governor Albert J. Wallace, included Mary Bowen, William Bowen's wife, pouring a tiny stream of Owens River water from a silver goblet onto the ground and proclaiming, "I christen thee Exposition Park."[114]

Right: Terra-cotta eagle and wreath detail from above the old entrance of the Natural History Museum. *Author photo*.

Below: Terra-cotta detail from the façade of the Natural History Museum. *Author photo*.

Opposite: The east side and original entrance to the Natural History Museum. Now patrons enter from the north side. *Author photo*.

Julia Bracken Wendt clay model for the *Spirit of History, Science and Art.* From the Year Book: Los Angeles Architectural Club, *1912.*

The final cost of the building was now estimated to be $250,000, and the contractor in charge was J.F. Atkinson. More details concerning the building were revealed, including the foyer's floor would be made of mosaic tiles, each wing would measure 50 by 110 feet and Julia Bracken Wendt was working on a sculpture, in her atelier, for the rotunda with the theme "The Spirit of History, Science and Art."[115]

In June 1911, the board of supervisors agreed to pay $7,500 for the Bracken Wendt statuary group. The sculpture was described in press reports as consisting of three eight-foot-tall bronze seminude figures holding aloft a globe "that will be illuminated in a manner not yet determined."[116] The pedestal made of Sienna marble was four feet high. Wendt was a Los Angeles resident who had done sculptural work for the Chicago and St. Louis expositions and for the City of Los Angeles.

Alfred F. Rosenheim, who was president of the Fine Arts League, stated that the key to all exhibits would be "practical and educational." Rosenheim was reported to be an influential force in the Los Angeles arts community, and one of the first exhibits the Fine Arts League was planning would be an "exhibition of paintings by California artists." Directors George F. Bovard and Alfred F. Rosenheim greeted guests when the building opened on November 6, 1913.

The Natural History Museum is listed in the National Register of Historic Places.

As noted by a January 7, 1915 article in the *Los Angeles Times*, Munsell's daughter, Elizabeth V. Munsell, was married in St. James Episcopal Church in South Pasadena to LeRoy Linnard. Only members of the immediate family were present. The bridegroom's best man was William Travenor, but the bride had no attendants. The bride was given away by her father, W.A.O. Munsell. After the ceremony, the bridal party went to the Midwick Country Club for a wedding supper.

In 1920, Munsell and Julia were living by themselves at 1970 El Molino in San Marino, but by 1930, they had moved to 2405 Ridgeway Road

Right: The *Spirit of History, Science and Art* in the rotunda of the Natural History Museum. The space and statue have been used in many movies, including *The Bonfire of the Vanities*. *Author photo.*

Below: The Natural History Museum of Los Angeles County, circa 1912. At that time, it was known as the Museum of History, Science and Art. *Courtesy of* Pacific Coast Architect.

also in San Marino. The 1930 census stated they owned the San Marino house, but Elizabeth, who claimed to be thirty when she was really thirty-two, was back living with Munsell and Julia, so her marriage must not have worked out. According to voter registration cards, by 1938, Munsell and Julia were living at 400 South Madison in Pasadena and both belonged to the Townsend Party. The Townsend Party advocated giving all U.S. citizens over the age of sixty $200 a month. Munsell eventually moved to Menominee, Wisconsin, to live with Elizabeth in 1939. He died there on April 22, 1944, and is buried, next to Julia and Elizabeth, at the Forest Home Cemetery in Milwaukee, Wisconsin.

Frank D. Hudson was a thirty-second-degree Mason and a member of the Architecture and Engineers Association and the Southern California chapter of the American Institute of Architects. He was president of the AIA Southern California chapter in 1910. Hudson also belonged to the Jonathan Club and the Los Angeles Country Club. He enjoyed playing golf, too. There are numerous news reports about his success on Los Angeles golf courses.

He died on March 16, 1941, at age seventy-three, from a heart attack at his San Marino home. His survivors were his wife, Harriet L. Hudson, and daughter, Mrs. J.S. (Doris) Woollacott. He is buried at Forest Lawn Memorial Park in Glendale, California.

6
ALBERT C. MARTIN

Albert C. Martin is what George V. Credle would consider an "academically trained architect." Credle wrote that the academically trained architect replaced "the builder architect who both designed and built as well as that of the gentleman architect working with a staff or draftsmen who were often simultaneously apprentices."[117] Martin also is the only major architect in Southern California who opened an architectural firm at the beginning of the twentieth century (1906) that is still in existence today, now known as AC Martin Partners.

Albert C. Martin was born in La Salle, Illinois, on September 16, 1879. His parents were John and Mary (née Carey) Martin, and his father ran a hardware store in La Salle. Along with the hardware store, John Martin also worked in furniture sales and undertaking. Albert had seven brothers and sisters, but the sibling who had the biggest effect on Martin's life was his brother Joseph. Joseph was an ordained priest and the first of the Martin clan to move to California.[118] After Albert graduated from the University of Illinois in 1902 with a degree in architectural engineering, Joseph urged his brother to venture west. Martin resisted. After graduation, Albert C. Martin first found employment working as a draftsman for Ketchum Iron Works in Indianapolis, Indiana, and stayed employed there for a little over a year before resigning. Next, he obtained a job at the Pennsylvania Railroad Company as a steel inspector. After he learned all he could about steel and iron construction, he quit that job and obtained employment at Cambria Steel in Johnstown, Pennsylvania, which became a branch of

U.S. Steel. He stayed at Cambria for a few months as a "designer and estimator of steel construction."[119] Finally, he must have felt he had acquired enough knowledge and was ready to move to California. Martin arrived in Los Angeles on January 6, 1904. Yet the big lure to California had to be an offer he received from Carl Leonardt to be superintendent of construction for Carl Leonardt and Company. It was one of the big construction firms in Los Angeles. Martin worked for Leonardt for a little over a year and then moved on to become Alfred F. Rosenheim's construction engineer.

Martin married Ventura County resident Carolyn Borchard on October 16, 1907, in Oxnard, California, and they had six children. The Martin home was located at 712 South Catalina Street in Los Angeles, which is south of Wilshire Boulevard and across the street from where the Ambassador Hotel would

Albert C. Martin. He worked as Alfred F. Rosenheim's engineer of construction for four years. *Courtesy of* Notables of the Southwest.

be built. Martin devoted some of his leisure time to coaching St. Vincent's College track team, which he enjoyed, as he was a hurdler at the University of Illinois.

Professionally, before Albert C. Martin worked as an architect, he worked as an engineer. Two buildings that have a confusing attribution, as a result, are the Hamburger Department Store and the Higgins Building. Alfred F. Rosenheim received the contract for the Hamburger Department Store (1906) and is listed as the architect of record for the building, but Rosenheim was "let go" and Martin took over the project. The Higgins Building (1910) is sometimes attributed to Martin, and he did work on the building as the engineer, but according to Robert Burdette's *Greater Los Angeles & Southern California Portraits & Personal Memoranda*, which was published in 1910—when all these people were alive—A.L. Haley was the architect of the Higgins Building.

Martin also was the structural engineer for the Second Church of Christ, Scientist on West Adams Boulevard in Los Angeles. Alfred F. Rosenheim was the architect of the building, and while construction commenced in 1908, it was not finished until 1910. Martin's role involved calculating how to construct the huge dome that graces the church and the necessary support it would require.

VENTURA COUNTY COURTHOUSE

In 1911 Ventura County, at the time known for its lima bean fields and lemon trees, needed a county courthouse. Since Ventura was rather remote, it's not surprising to see a newspaper refer to the design of the new Ventura County Courthouse as "imposing" and almost question the need for such a formal building in a rural area. The reporter quickly corrected himself and endorsed the new courthouse. Once the idea sunk in, he wrote, the building would be "a credit to the seat of government of the prosperous lima bean section."[120]

Plans called for the courthouse to have a frontage of 280 feet and a depth of 95 feet. Style-wise it was Classical Revival with a row of Doric columns facing Poli Street. The building cost was estimated to be $200,000, and by April 23, 1911, bid requests for the excavation had gone out. Excavation was to be finished by July 15, and March 1, 1912, was set as the completion date of the courthouse. They were very optimistic.

The site was deemed noteworthy because it sat on a ridge that looked out over the city and beyond to the Pacific Ocean but was still within the business

Ventura County Court House. *Courtesy of* The Architect.

district. The fireproof nature of the building was emphasized along with the "reinforced concrete skeleton of columns, floors and roof inclosed [*sic*] with heavy brick walls."[121] Granite and white glazed terra cotta cover the exterior of the building with interior stairways of marble. Plans called for important papers and books to be housed in rooms with hollow metal doors, metal windows and metal trim to ensure against fire. Offices had maple floors and all other woodwork throughout the building was oak. When built the main courtroom had a twenty-eight-foot coffered ceiling and ornamental plaster beams. The courthouse was dedicated on July 12, 1913, sixteen months later than expected.

Martin invented a reinforced concrete construction process called the Lund-Martin system, which he used on many of his projects, and in 1915, he was the president of the Southern California chapter of the American Institute of Architects.

Martin's 1916 commission for a theater and office complex continued a trend of encircling a large theater with an even larger office building, a design concept that would continue through the 1920s and into the early 1930s.

EDISON BUILDING AND MILLION DOLLAR THEATRE

The Stability Building Company was the developer of the twelve-story Edison Building, which would house Grauman's Million Dollar Theatre on the ground floor. The Stability Building Company's president was Homer Laughlin Jr. His father, Homer Laughlin Sr., founded a pottery company in Ohio that produced dishware for the home. Homer Laughlin Sr. moved his family to Los Angeles in 1897, where he set up a real estate development business.

Sid Grauman announced in December 1916 that he had signed a ten-year lease for the theater, and the estimated cost of Grauman's lease for the ten-year period was $400,000. Albert C. Martin was the architect, and he designed the building in the Spanish Renaissance style. A press report stated the lobby would be entered "through an old Spanish doorway that will rise to the height of several stories forming the dominate architectural feature of the building."[122] The lobby was to be decorated in bronze and marble, and Martin had designed it so it would be wide and spacious to "avoid the jamming at the entrance so disconcerting to theater patrons."[123]

Grauman said of the theater,

> *I consider Los Angeles one of the best show towns in the country and I think we have picked out the ideal location in Los Angeles for the kind of high-class motion-picture theater my associates and myself have long contemplated establishing here. We shall give a high-class picture programme and concerts of the highest order every afternoon and night.*[124]

A year later, in December 1917, Albert C. Martin put architect William L. Wollett in charge of the interior design, and Wollett created an interior that incorporated elements from not only Byzantine treasures but old Mexican cathedrals as well. Wollett's goal was to create a "temple of mirth." The exact seating was listed as 2,300, with 1,300 seats on the ground floor and 1,000 in the balcony, though a newspaper article posted the day after the theater's opening stated there were 2,500 seats. The main auditorium's dimensions were 103 feet wide by 108 feet long.

Two days before Christmas 1917, the lighting for the theater, both inside and outside, was detailed in an article titled "New Lighting Wonders." At the time of the opening Grauman used electric light bulbs to illuminate the exterior but unlike other contemporary theaters, Grauman also planned to

Edison Building and Million Dollar Theatre near the end of construction. *Courtesy of the California History Room, California State Library, Sacramento, California.*

Million Dollar Theatre marquee. *Author photo.*

use searchlights. The searchlights, strategically placed at the corner of Third and Broadway, would illuminate "the entire building, creating a flashing brilliance that will be seen far over the city."[125] These klieg lights would also illuminate the "great statues standing in niches over the wide arches of the lower floor—all will be swept by recurrent rays of powerful light."[126] The lighting in the auditorium would be indirect light hidden in coves while

Right: Million Dollar Theatre façade detail. The statue appears to be the Egyptian god Thoth. *Author photo*.

Below: Edison Building elaborate cornice detail. *Author photo*.

Edison Building's ornate side entrance with steer horn skulls and an eagle. *Author photo*.

in the mezzanine, plans called for dim chandeliers in a style reminiscent of feudal lighting to give patrons the impression they were walking down old castle corridors. Originally, a six-foot chandelier was the primary light source in the main lobby.

Grauman's Million Dollar Theatre program. The building is floating within the proscenium arch. *Author's collection.*

The balcony was one of the engineering feats detailed in news reports because of its 110-foot span. At the time, it was so unusual the City Building Department required that a test be completed in which 1.5 million pounds were placed upon the span, to allay safety concerns, before the city would approve it, which it did. (1.5 million pounds sounds unbelievable, but it was the amount given by newspapers days before the building opened.)

Opening night on February 1, 1918, featured an organ recital by Jesse Crawford and music from Grauman's thirty-piece symphony orchestra, led by conductor Rudolph Kopp. The opening night feature film was *The Silent Man* starring William S. Hart. Hart was there in person along with numerous other stars who came out for the event, including Charlie Chaplin, Douglas Fairbanks, Mary Pickford, Sessue Hayakawa, Roscoe (Fatty) Arbuckle, Wallace Reid, Charles Ray, Anita King, Constance Talmadge, Mary Miles Minter, Mae Murray, Bryant Washburn, William Desmond and Lillian Gish. Major directors in attendance included D.W. Griffith, Jesse Lasky, Mack Sennett, Thomas Ince and Lois Weber. It was said of the film colony, "For the most part the actors and actresses and directors who attended were in evening dress, which lent a brilliant metropolitan air to the assemblage."[127]

The theater's opening was a society event. Those invited by Grauman to attend included William May Garland, Homer Laughlin Jr., D.A. Hamburger, Mr. and Mrs. Albert C. Martin, Mr. and Mrs. Harry Chandler, Mr. and Mrs. I.W. Hellman Jr. and Mr. and Mrs. John Hyde Braly.

The *Los Angeles Times* reported, "In the loges and all over the immense auditorium, hundreds of richly gowned society women beamed their approval on the opening offering. Most of the ladies wore demi-toilettes of velvets, brocades and rich silks. A number were noticed in smart street dress and a few were in full evening dress."[128]

The Edison Building and the Million Dollar Theatre are listed in the National Register of Historic Places.

Martin's next venture involved a church and his possible legacy.

ST. VINCENT'S CHURCH

The sketches Albert C. Martin drew up for St. Vincent's Church were approved and accepted in December 1922 by the pastor of St. Vincent's Parish, Reverend James H. MacRoberts, and the Right Reverend John J. Cantwell, who was the bishop of the Los Angeles diocese. The new church was to be situated at the northwest corner of Figueroa and West Adams Streets. Martin stated the working drawings would be ready by June 1, 1923, and the church would cost approximately $500,000.

Edward and Estelle Doheny, who lived nearby on Chester Place, donated $250,000 toward the erection of the church at the outset and, a few months later, upped their donation to $500,000. This was followed by another donation of $100,000.

Doheny, who had an estimated worth in 1925 of over $100 million, would be implicated in the Teapot Dome scandal in 1925, prosecuted by the federal government on corruption charges (bribing Interior Secretary Albert Bacon Fall) but found not guilty even though the person who accepted Doheny's money, Fall, was found guilty of accepting a bribe.

On May 12, 1923, Albert C. Martin, Bishop Cantwell, Edward L. Doheny and John Henry Dockweiller announced the final architectural drawings had been accepted and approved and work would commence within ninety days. Based on the final plans, the estimated cost of St. Vincent's was now $1.5 million.

The groundbreaking occurred five months later on October 13, 1923. The design of the church is in the Spanish Churrigueresque style and placed at an angle to the intersection so any future buildings on adjacent lots would not obscure the building. The church contains a cruciform plan inside, and the nave is 200 feet long by 65 feet wide. It can accommodate 1,800. The interior is decorated with ornamental plaster, and most entrances have stone trimmings and wood ornamentation. Marble and tile is used on the floors, and marble and stone is used for the altar and sanctuary. Biblical scenes are depicted in the art glass throughout the building. The steeple soars to 150 feet, contains bells and an observation platform. The laying of the cornerstone took place on July 18, 1924, and the building was dedicated on Easter Sunday, April 12, 1925.

The building's consecration occurred on October 23 and October 26, 1930. Inside the booklet for the consecration are photographs of Estelle and Edward Doheny. Opposite their photographs is an ornately drawn cartouche with the inscription: "With deepfelt and sincere gratitude this programme is

St. Vincent's Church, 1920s. *Courtesy of the California History Room, California State Library, Sacramento, California.*

dedicated to Mr. and Mrs. Edward Laurence Doheny through whose faith and munificence was builded [*sic*] this majestic temple to the living God."

According to the consecration program, Cram and Ferguson of Boston designed the High Altar, which is the main altar parishioners see when walking down the church's center aisle.

St. Vincent's Church today. *Author photo.*

St. Vincent's Church altar, which was designed by Cram and Ferguson. *From St. Vincent's consecration program.*

The church was declared Los Angeles Historic Cultural Monument No. 90 on July 21, 1971.

At one time, Albert C. Martin thought St. Vincent's Church would be the building he would be remembered for, but Martin's place in the pantheon of Southern California architects would be tied to an even bigger project that involved Martin teaming up with John C. Austin and John Parkinson to form the Associated Architects and erecting the new city hall for Los Angeles.

In 1928, Martin was part of the defense in a case that involved actress Mae Murray. Murray was a silent film star who starred in *Modern Love* (1918), *The Gilded Lily* (1921), *Peacock Alley* (1922) and *The Merry Widow* (1925). She was the girl with the bee-stung lips and was quoted as saying after watching *Sunset Boulevard*, "None of us floozies were that nuts!"

Murray was in a dispute over a house she had purchased from an architect named John Francis Donovan. The purchase included furnishings. Murray claimed there were problems with the house and some of the furnishings had been replaced with inferior items.

Albert C. Martin was brought to court by the defense and testified that not only was the residence well designed and constructed beyond reproach but that the windows were almost burglarproof as well. The courtroom erupted with laughter on numerous occasions when Murray's attorney, W.I. Gilbert, questioned Martin because Martin talked at length and was determined to prove his point no matter how much time it took. Gilbert became frustrated with Martin, appealed to Judge Ballard for some succinctness and asked that the witness respond with either a straightforward "yes" or "no." Martin must have tried the judge's patience, too, because Judge Ballard asked Martin to condense his answers.[129] Murray won the court case and was awarded a financial settlement, but the bad blood between Murray and the architect John Francis Donovan didn't end there. After the trial, Donovan accused Murray of "breaking and entering," perjury and kidnapping and drugging his chauffer, so the two ended up back in court.

Martin continued to work in the architectural field throughout the 1930s and into the 1940s. One of the last buildings of note done under his watch was the May Company Building on Wilshire Boulevard in Los Angeles. On October 20, 1938, Tom May, executive vice president of the May Company, announced his company would build a five-story department store on the northeast corner of Wilshire and Fairfax and the building would cost in excess of $2 million. The store would not only have parking for six hundred cars but also house salons and a restaurant on the roof. Albert C. Martin was the main architect on the project and assisted by Samuel A. Marx, who was Tom May's brother-in-law.

In the book *AC Martin Partners: One Hundred years of Architecture*, the Wilshire Boulevard May Company store is described:

> *The finished five-story steel frame building was sheathed in black granite on the lower story, with the uper walls covered with Texas limestone, a neutral tone meant to draw the eye directly to a curved plane of gold-leaf Italian glass tile, set into bowed black granite fins. This corner focal point served not only as the May Company building's signpost, but also identified the main entrance.*[130]

The store opened on September 7, 1939, six days after Hitler invaded Poland. Morton J. May, head of the company, was still optimistic about the future and said on opening day that Los Angeles was a great place for opportunity, economic growth and family happiness.

The May Company store on Wilshire Boulevard closed fifty-three years later, in 1992, but the edifice, still iconic in its streamlined modern design, will be part of the new Academy of Motion Picture Arts and Sciences Museum slated to open in 2019.

Albert C. Martin began to spend less time in his office and, by the end of World War II, turned over most of the day-to-day running of the firm to his sons, Albert Jr. and Ed.

In the book *Courthouses of California*, there is an anecdote that gives readers some insight into how Martin spent his later years. It appears he was revisiting his work—in this instance, the Ventura County Courthouse. "In the mid-1950s, Albert Martin, by then an old man, visited the chambers of the board of supervisors unannounced. Introducing himself—no one recognized him—Martin told the board that, after a long career, the Ventura County courthouse was one of the buildings in which he took 'particular pride.'"[131]

In 1959, Martin received the Los Angeles Chamber of Commerce Man of Achievement Award for "his outstanding accomplishments and contributions in fine architecture and in the development of building materials designed to withstand earthquakes and to solve unusual difficult building problems."[132]

Albert C. Martin was eighty when he died on April 9, 1960. Martin lived a long, full life and left a lengthy list of children and grandchildren as his survivors. His wife of fifty-two years, Carolyn, had died the year before. Both are buried at Holy Cross Cemetery in Culver City, California.

7

MEYER & HOLLER:
THE MILWAUKEE BUILDING COMPANY

The Milwaukee Building Company, which was founded by Mendel Meyer in 1906, went from being a startup to enormously successful and then it slowly faded away. Philip W. Holler's rise within the Milwaukee Building Company from "no role in the company" to vice president to "no role" again parallels the company itself.

Philip W. Holler was born on January 4, 1869, in Indiana. His parents, both Indiana natives, were Christian and Mary, and Holler had an elder sister also named Mary and a younger brother Ed. Holler was a farmer in Indiana and married Lily Sherfey on November 15, 1894. Within a few years, the couple had two sons, Wesley and Albert, and the family moved to Los Angeles in the first decade of the twentieth century. According to census records, they were still married in 1910, but sometime between 1910 and 1913, Holler divorced Lily, and he married Mary J. Feerrar on September 15, 1913. This marriage did not last either. According to a newspaper report from March 1919, Holler, "vice president of a large building company," was charged with desertion by his second wife, Mary Holler, "after a married life of six years."[133]

Mendel Meyer was born on October 7, 1874, in Los Angeles. His parents, both from Germany, were Samuel and Johanna. Meyer had a brother named Gabe and a sister named Rose. According to his obituary, Meyer was a graduate of the "old Los Angeles High School," but Meyer never attended college or received a degree from any institution of higher education.

Meyer married Mable M. Gray in Los Angeles on January 4, 1915. He was forty years old when he married for the first time. Mable had been married before and had a son named Miles.

Two major projects the Milwaukee Building Company undertook before 1920 were the Charlie Chaplin Studios in Los Angeles and the Thomas Ince Studios in Culver City. Announced on October 16, 1917, the Chaplin project was situated on five acres of land Chaplin bought from R.S. McClellan. Sunset Boulevard was the lot line on the north, La Brea Boulevard on the west and De Longpre Street on the east. Chaplin's purchase included the McClellan mansion, which was located near Sunset Boulevard, and Chaplin planned to use it as his home. Orange trees covered the rest of the acreage. Six quaint one- and two-story English-style buildings were designed to run down La Brea Boulevard, while the sound stages and dressing rooms were built away from the street and out of view of motorists. The cost was approximately $100,000. Chaplin began to use the studio at the end of January 1918.

The Chaplin Studios are currently the home of the Jim Henson Studios.

Announced on November 17, 1917, the Ince Studios project was bigger than the Chaplin project. It involved eleven acres, twelve to eighteen concrete buildings that included open air and glass stages, a swimming pool and an outlay of between $200,000 and $500,000. The acreage Ince bought fronted Washington Boulevard in Culver City. Ince stated he was leaving his oceanside studio, out near Malibu, because he had become tired of having to deal with the low cloud cover over the studio, which caused delays in shooting.

The Ince Studios were ready by Christmas 1918, but Thomas Ince would only use his namesake studios for six years before his unfortunate death, which was the result of a trip aboard William Randolph Hearst's *Oneida* in 1924. Producer David Selznick eventually moved onto the Ince lot, and the Ince administration building can be seen in the opening credits of *Gone with the Wind*. In 2014, the studio lot sold for $85 million to Hackman Capital Partners, an investment firm.

The team of Meyer & Holler was able to design and construct these pre-1920s film studios quickly, but that's not all the firm did. It also provided interior design services and arranged building loans for clients. The loan aspect of the business would be the duo's undoing and would lead to the company's collapse when a famous film director sued because he claimed he had been cheated.

Before that happened, the Milwaukee Building Company had a prosperous decade in which it constructed three Hollywood landmarks.

THE HOLLYWOOD ATHLETIC CLUB

In September 1921, plans to build the Hollywood Athletic Club were announced at the Hollywood Public Library following a meeting of the charter members of the club. The members stated they wanted to build an athletic club somewhere between Cahuenga and Highland and probably on Sunset. The total outlay the club planned to expend was $200,000, which included the cost of the land.

By the following April, the Hollywood Athletic Club had signed up 635 members with a goal of reaching a membership of 1,000. Leadership hoped to pick up more members by persuading local businessmen and prominent members of the community to join. Plans for the new building were drawn up and completed by the Milwaukee Building Company. The design was in the "Italian villa style of architecture, which both the architects and officials of the club believe is particularly adapted to this country."[134] The new Hollywood Athletic Club would have 200 feet of frontage on Sunset Boulevard and 157 feet along Hudson Avenue. The plot, purchased for $35,000, had increased in value and was worth $50,000 a few months later. Amenities in the new facility according to the original plans would include a gymnasium, handball courts, "swimming tanks," lockers, showers, a barbershop, banquet halls, reading and writing rooms, a café, a billiard room and lounge rooms.

It was noted in a *Times* article that Meyer & Holler "have the contract for architectural design, engineering, construction, decorating and furnishings. All furniture, draperies, carpets and lighting fixtures are being specially designed, and with infinite care is being taken the interior decorations, the object being to produce harmony in design, furnishings and color scheme."[135]

By December 1923, construction had been completed. The measurements had changed on Hudson Street with the frontage increasing from 157 feet to 210 feet. The athletic club was two stories with a nine-story tower, which contained fifty-four rooms for "bachelor" members for a grand total of eleven stories.

The exterior of the building was cream-colored stucco, and it was graced with a red tile roof. When built, the interior rooms had a Florentine design, and some of the main rooms were copies of Florentine rooms in European palaces. The seating capacity in the dining room was three hundred, and a modern Pompeian decoration was used in the game room. The final breakdown of cost was $200,000 for the land, which had increased six

Right: Hollywood Athletic Club. *Author photo*.

Below: Hollywood Athletic Club grill with initials of the club over entrance. *Author photo*.

times, from what it had originally cost, and $800,000 for the building and furnishings for a grand total of $1,000,000.

Opening day was January 12, 1924, for members, their families and friends. A Hawaiian orchestra provided music to accompany the buffet luncheon, which was held in the dining room, and notable Hawaiian Duke Kahanamoku was featured in an aquatic exhibition. Part of the opening day festivities included an exhibition on the Roman rings, a side horse exhibition, tumbling and acrobatics, feats of strength, horizontal and parallel bar work, swimming, water polo, diving and *comedy* diving. Comedy diving was about horseplay and gimmicks. It included men dressed in women's bathing attire, jump ropes and diving board mayhem, with the diving being similar to a pratfall.

The Hollywood Athletic Club won an award in 1925 from the Southern California chapter of the American Institute of Architects in the category "multiple dwellings of the club type."

Meyer & Holler's status in Los Angeles went up even higher with their next major project.

THE CHINESE THEATRE

The most famous theater in the world might be the Chinese Theatre, but when the theater was first announced, it was clouded in secrecy. Sid Grauman, who had built the Hollywood Egyptian Theatre in 1922, was mentioned as being the man behind this latest theater project in Hollywood, but that was one of the few details offered. The future location of the theater was given, on Hollywood Boulevard between Orange Drive and Orchard Avenue along with the names of the architects, Meyer & Holler, who would handle the architecture, construction, decoration and engineering. Yet prominently situated in the initial announcement was the unusual statement that the architectural details of Grauman's new theater would remain undisclosed.[136]

At the groundbreaking ceremonies held on January 5, 1926, Anna Mae Wong, whose credits include *The Thief of Bagdad* (1924), handed Norma Talmadge, one of the famous Talmadge sisters, a spade to turn over the first mounds of earth for the Chinese Theatre. Joseph M. Schenck, head of United Artists, and Sid Grauman each said a few words as part of the festivities, and after they spoke, Chinese women immediately served everyone tea.

By October 1926, the style of the building had become a well-known secret, and many newspaper articles openly referred to it as Grauman's Chinese Theatre. One article stated that Meyer & Holler had set up a laboratory, on-site, to produce miniature models of the sculpture that would be placed around the theater. The models were studied for correctness in scale before the large versions were cast.

Also noted in the same newspaper article, not directly but indirectly, was that Grauman wanted the theater to be authentic and he consulted with those who had knowledge of Chinese culture. Liu Yu Chang, a renowned expert on Chinese art, looked over the models at Grauman's request and approved them.[137]

Yet secrecy still prevailed. The entrance to the forecourt was closed off and hidden behind a high screen, which made only the upper portion of the theater visible from the street. An article titled "Secrecy Marks Building" relayed that the reason everything was done in secrecy was because Grauman wanted to provide his first night's audience with spectacle and surprise.[138]

With the opening of the theater growing near, Grauman and Cecil B. DeMille announced the opening attraction would be DeMille's *King of Kings* featuring H.B. Warner, Joseph Schildkraut, Bryant Washburn and Sally Rand.

Times writer Marquis Busby gushed three days before the theater's opening that the event was one of the most important affairs in recent theatrical history.[139] Much of what Busby wrote was hyperbole, but some of the information he relayed was interesting. Busby stated the Chinese's stage, which had the dimensions of one hundred feet wide by forty-six feet deep, was, at that time, the third-largest stage in the United States. Only the stages of the New York Hippodrome and the Los Angeles Shrine Auditorium were bigger. Busby wrote the Chinese's pagoda's roof was ninety feet above the forecourt. The theater had an independent power plant, which provided electricity for the theater along with its own heating and ventilation system. The walls that encircled the courtyard were forty feet high. The theater seated 2,200 people on a single floor. This was Grauman's fifth theater in the Los Angeles area. His other four theaters were the Million Dollar, Rialto and Metropolitan (all in downtown Los Angeles) and the Hollywood Egyptian, which also was a Meyer & Holler building.

The premiere and grand opening took place on May 18, 1927. By 5:00 p.m., fans waiting on the sidewalks were ten deep, and by 9:00 p.m., it took half an hour to walk a single block. Norma Talmadge, at Grauman's request, put her hand and footprints in cement on opening night and started a tradition

Above: Chinese Theatre, circa 1930. *Opposite*: Chinese Theatre. *Courtesy of the California History Room, California State Library, Sacramento, California.*

that continues to today. Inside the theater, D.W. Griffith spoke first and regaled the audience with a history of the theater. Not the Chinese Theatre, but of the history of the theater in general, and how through the dark ages, when there was no theater, mankind withdrew into itself. Cecil B. DeMille, who spoke about his production of *King of Kings*, followed Griffith. After he finished, he handed the proceedings over to Will Hayes, who was there to introduce Mary Pickford. Pickford, who was dressed in a golden gown of sequins, was handed an electric button by Hayes. She looked at it and smiled before she pushed the button. With that gesture, America's sweetheart formally opened the Chinese

Theatre.[140] It is not clear exactly what she opened since everyone was already in the theater, so the "button pushing" may have been a symbolic gesture, but she could have opened the curtain.

Edwin Schallert, who covered the event for the *Times*, said the theater was filled with beauty and he expected tourists would make a special effort to see it.[141]

D.W. Griffith wrote to Grauman a few days later to express his admiration. He said rather imperially that artists, or someone with an artist's soul, were the only ones who could truly appreciate the monumental beauty of the theater. Then he wisely predicted that the theater would be world famous.[142]

The Chinese Theatre was declared Los Angeles Historic Cultural Monument No. 55 on June 5, 1968.

HOLLYWOOD FIRST NATIONAL BANK

The Hollywood First National Bank is on countless postcards from the 1920s, 1930s, 1940s and 1950s. Whenever a photographer wanted a photograph looking down Hollywood Boulevard, he or she usually included this bank as a demarcation point. It was originally known by two different names: Pacific Southwest Trust and Savings Bank, or Los Angeles First National Trust and Savings Bank.

The first mention of this landmark bank is in a four-paragraph newspaper article dated July 24, 1927. The article reported that rapidly growing Hollywood would soon have a new $750,000 building designed for the Pacific Southwest Trust and Savings Bank and it would be located on the northeast corner of Hollywood and Highland.[143]

A follow-up article in October still referred to the bank as the Pacific Southwest Trust and Savings Bank. This article stated that the old bank had been demolished, the site had been cleared and excavation work was set to begin. The architectural firm Meyer & Holler is mentioned as the designers of the building and in charge of the new bank's construction. It reported the building would be six stories and have a tower of 190 feet. Gladding-McBean & Co. was awarded the contract for the terra cotta, and it was to supply 150 tons of terra cotta for the facing. Above the main floor, the plans called for 127 offices of various sizes; the building would be stepped back and be steel framed. This article erroneously reported the building would be located on the northwest corner of Hollywood and Highland.[144]

Six weeks later, in a lengthy article that discussed various bank projects in the Los Angeles region, the Meyer & Holler bank is mentioned, but this time it is referred to as Los Angeles First National Trust and Savings Bank.[145] Everything else rings right though: it's located at Hollywood and Highland, it's a bank and office building, the previous bank was torn down,

Above: First National Bank of Hollywood entrance pediment. Note the bees and honeycomb. *Author photo*.

Right: First National Bank of Hollywood tower with eagles, cranes, lions and pineapples. *Author photo*.

First National Bank of Hollywood at the corner of Hollywood and Highland Boulevards.
Author photo.

it's steel and concrete, it's six stories and has a 190-foot tower, the façade would be terra cotta and the design allows for flood lighting at night.

On July 1, 1928, less than a year after announced, the building was completed. In a newspaper article accompanied by a photo, it is referred to as the Los Angeles First National Trust and Savings Bank. Tenants had already moved into their offices, but the Hollywood branch of Los Angeles First National would not have its formal opening until September 8 at the earliest. The *Times* declared, "The building, because of its tower construction, is one of the outstanding edifices in Hollywood."[146]

THE KING VIDOR JUDGMENT

In the early 1930s, the Milwaukee Building Company had to deal with an unfortunate situation that appeared from out of the past. King Vidor, the director of *The Big Parade* (1925), *The Crowd* (1928) and eventually *The Fountainhead* (1949), had filed a lawsuit against the Milwaukee Building Company. In the early 1920s, Vidor, along with his father, C.S., hired the Milwaukee Building Company to locate and purchase a five-acre tract of land off Santa Monica Boulevard for the purpose of building a motion picture studio for them. Vidor and his father claimed they were overcharged $32,608.20 when they undertook this venture. The vast majority of the amount the Vidors were seeking was due to what they claimed was an excessive interest rate. On May 8, 1932, superior court judge Dailey S. Stafford ruled in favor of the Vidors and awarded them $27,799.08 with interest back to September 1, 1922.[147]

No reaction from Meyer or Holler was recorded, but a judgment that size must have been difficult to deal with—especially in the middle of the Depression. In today's dollars, it is equal to $496,000.

The firm of Meyer & Holler trudged along during the Depression, but the firm had lost its air of invincibility. It was like a zeppelin slowly crashing to the ground. The ruling definitely had an effect on their business. It moved from the elegant Wright & Callender Building where it had luxurious offices for twenty years to a location on West Washington Boulevard next to the railroad tracks.

Holler lived with his sister Mary Cunningham for a time in the 1930s and then rented a farmhouse on Balboa Avenue where he spent his last years. Holler died on November 24, 1942 at age seventy-three and was buried at Valhalla Memorial Park in North Hollywood. He was survived by his sons Wesley and Albert.

Meyer was sixty-five in 1939 and retired sometime after that. It had been seven years since the King Vidor judgment, but he probably hadn't paid it off by then. In 1939, he made only $3,421 and was living in a $60 a month apartment.

After he retired, Meyer lived in both Los Angeles and Glendale before he moved up to Santa Barbara in November 1954. Meyer lived in Santa Barbara's California Hotel, which was owned by Meyer's stepson, Miles. Mendel Meyer died on April 1, 1955, at eighty and was buried at the Santa Barbara Cemetery. Upon his death, Meyer left a widow, Mable Miles Meyer, and stepson, Miles R. Gray.

8

JULIA MORGAN

The *San Francisco Chronicle* ran a short article about Julia Morgan in 1901 regarding her training in Paris. "She Qualifies in Paris as Architect" was the title. The article states, "Morgan, of Oakland, has won the distinction of being the first American woman to graduate from the architectural section of the Ecole des Beaux Arts [*sic*] of Paris."[148] The coursework at the École was difficult, according to the *Chronicle*, and while other American women had attempted to complete and graduate from the architectural program, none had succeeded.

While in Paris, Morgan received training in the office of Chaussemiche, who was a well-known architect in the city. When asked to comment on Morgan's achievement, Chaussemiche responded,

> *She will make a very good architect. Her taste in ornamentation, however, will require correction. In common with her compatriots, Miss Morgan mixes styles a little too much, but this slight fault will pass away and I have no doubt she will succeed very well in her country. I would have no hesitation in confiding to her the erection of a building, as in the science of the profession she is far superior to half of her male comrades. It is true that the objection can be made that a woman cannot well climb scaffolds to oversee the work or come into contact with the laborers and mechanics but an architect's functions do not consist exclusively of those disagreeable duties. His office work, such as preparing plans and sketches, is more important and for this women are well suited.*[149]

She had to wait to obtain her certificate, though, because even though she finished all the coursework in two years, the École withheld her certificate, maybe, hoping she would simply go away. Not deterred, Morgan reenrolled in classes, entered an architectural competition that was underway at the École and won first prize. The school was probably annoyed with her persistence, but it must have also realized it had no alternative but to award her the certificate she had earned. When Morgan returned to the Bay Area, she went to work for John Galen Howard, who was happy with her work. He said to a colleague that he had hired a great designer who "he didn't have to pay anything because she is a woman."[150]

Julia Morgan. *Courtesy of the Julia Morgan Papers, Special Collections and Archives, California Polytechnic State University.*

This is the male attitude Julia Morgan had to deal with throughout her career.

Julia Morgan was born in San Francisco on January 20, 1872. Her parents were Charles Bill and Eliza Woodland Morgan. She had three brothers—Parmalee, Avery and Pardiner—and a sister named Emma. She graduated from Oakland High School in 1890 and received a bachelor of science degree in civil engineering from the University of California in 1894. She then went to Paris, at the urging of Bernard Maybeck, who was her mentor while at the University of California, and attempted to gain access to the École des Beaux-Arts, which was already under pressure to admit women. She arrived in Paris in 1896 and gained admittance in 1898, which was the first year the École admitted women to the architectural program.

With her certificate in her hand, back in the United States, Morgan struck out on her own in 1904 to become the "first woman licensed to practice architecture in California."[151] A story that reveals Morgan's stamina and determination comes from her nephew Morgan North, who said, "She often worked seven days a week, 10 to 15 hours a day. Before she had a car and driver she used to complain that she needed only four hours sleep a night but the cable car rested six."[152]

The dedication of the YWCA administration building occurred on October 9, 1922. The evening began with an all-girl processional singing "Hymn of Lights." First Methodist's Pastor Merle N. Smith then gave the invocation. More singing followed Pastor Smith, this time under the direction of community chorus leader Arthur Farwell. The presentation of the key to the building was the next event in the evening's program. Local YWCA president Mrs. George R. Stewart received the key from Mary Huggins Gamble.

Gamble's presentation invoked many responses. After all scheduled to speak spoke, everyone bowed his or her head for a dedication prayer given by Reverend Dr. Leslie E. Learned of Pasadena's All Saint's Church. Choral singing followed the prayer, and this singing closed the ceremony.

Not including the site, the administration building, which is three stories, cost $120,000 and is constructed of reinforced concrete. In the Spanish Colonial style, the building contains general offices, committee rooms, three clubrooms, an assembly room, a library, an infirmary, forty-six bedrooms, a cafeteria and a kitchen.

A feature of the building highlighted by the YWCA was its "utility room." This was a space provided for young women to use if they were caught in a

Pasadena YWCA, which is currently unoccupied. *Author photo*.

thunderstorm or their clothes become soiled in any way. In the utility room, young women could slip out of their clothes, wash them, dry them and be back on their way in no time.

A second unit containing a swimming pool and gymnasium was under construction when the administration building dedication took place. The building that housed the gymnasium and pool was threatened with demolition in the late 1980s when a plan was hatched to have the YMCA and the YWCA remain separate but use the same facility with separate entrances. The general manager of the YMCA said both YWCA buildings were obsolete and inefficient, and under a 1980s scheme, the building housing the gymnasium and pool would be demolished and the Morgan administration building enlarged. The plan failed to pass a city council vote, and before the buildings were destroyed (or altered), both were bought through eminent domain. As of this writing, they sit empty, awaiting renovation and a new use.

The Pasadena YWCA is listed in the National Register of Historic Places.

HOLLYWOOD STUDIO CLUB

Mary Pickford, Constance Adams DeMille, Norma Talmadge and ZaSu Pitts were some of the women at the groundbreaking ceremonies for Morgan's Hollywood project called the Hollywood Studio Club. Norma Talmadge, one of the biggest contributors to the venture, eagerly attended. Mary Pickford was the main speaker. ZaSu Pitts, who stayed at the club when she first arrived in Hollywood, was an enthusiastic booster. Julia Morgan made an appearance and Constance DeMille, assisted by May Parker, who was president of the club, started the steam shovel and turned the first loads of dirt.

The Hollywood Studio Club had been around since 1916 when a Hollywood librarian, Eleanor B. Jones, noticed young starlets hanging around the library "night after night in preference to attending the beach cafes or wandering around the streets."[160] After talking with the women, Jones realized that a safe place was needed for young women who came to Hollywood looking for work in the movie industry. Jones enlisted the aid of William C. DeMille, Lula Warrington and Bessie Ida Ginsberg to create such a place. The group approached several studios and the Hollywood Board of Trade and requested seed money to rent a home that could be used as a club for these young women from various parts of the country.

Hollywood Studio Club with stenciled name. *Author photo.*

Jones and her supporters received substantial contributions and rented an immense Greek Revival house on Carlos Avenue, but quickly, the Hollywood Studio Club outgrew the house, even though it was enormous, and needed a bigger facility. It was then that a fundraising campaign was undertaken to raise money for a new building. In an article the day before the groundbreaking ceremony, it was reported that since the YWCA had raised the funds, it would control the club.

Three months before the opening of the building, Julia Morgan spoke with Myra Nye for Nye's What Women are Doing column.

Julia Morgan described the building as a combination of styles that included French, Italian and Spanish influences. Combined together, they could be labeled as Mediterranean with a bit of Moorish coloring thrown in. Large windows and glass doors let in the light from the street, and one set of doors led out to a patio with a fountain. There was an ancient-looking fireplace in the living room along with a private dining room, a bigger dining room that could accommodate 150 diners, a library, reception rooms and a stage, all on the first floor. The second and third floors had balconies and sixty-six rooms for the female lodgers.[161]

Located at 1215 Lodi Place, the club had its grand opening on May 7, 1926. The dedication, which had over five hundred people in attendance, began at 4:30 p.m. in the club's auditorium. A prayer began the ceremony followed by remarks from Constance DeMille and film producer Charles Christie. The club was designed to be a home for female film industry employees and a social center. Each woman would receive a room and two meals a day for fifteen dollars a week. Many of the rented rooms were named after film stars who had contributed money to the building fund.

A long list of Hollywood actresses lived at the Hollywood Studio Club. Some of the biggest were Kim Novak, Marilyn Monroe, Linda Darnell and 1956 Academy Award winner Dorothy Malone. One notable writer who lived at the club was Ayn Rand, author of *The Fountainhead* and *Atlas Shrugged*.

The Hollywood Studio Club was declared Los Angeles Historic Cultural Monument No. 175 on May 4, 1977.

In 1928, Morgan had a medical procedure that ended badly. She had an inner ear infection, which had plagued her since childhood, so the surgery she selected involved removing the inner ear. During the operation, the ear surgeon accidently severed a facial nerve, which caused Morgan to have speech and facial issues similar to what an individual who has had a stroke experiences. Despite the botched operation, Morgan continued to work and

Hollywood Studio Club entrance. The breezeway above the entrance was unfortunately filled in. *Author photo.*

Hollywood Studio Club. The Hollywood Studio Club encircles this patio. *Author photo.*

did not blame the surgeon despite having balance, face and speech problems for the rest of her life.

According to the *American Institute of Architects Journal*, Morgan was a member of the American Institute of Architects (Northern California chapter) beginning in 1921 and was an emeritus member beginning in 1949, though from all accounts she seemed to shun participation in architectural organizations.

Julia Morgan designed more than seven hundred buildings during her career, which lasted until the early 1950s. William Randolph Hearst was the only journalist she spoke to on a regular basis. Morgan did not like to post her name at job sites, avoided publicity and never drew more than $10,000 a year in salary. Morgan's best-known buildings include Hearst Castle in San Simeon, a Mission Revival–style campanile at Mills College in Oakland, St. John's Presbyterian Church in Berkeley and the Asilomar Conference Center in Pacific Grove, California.

Julia Morgan never married and died at her home on February 2, 1957. She was eighty-five years old. She is buried at Mountain View Cemetery in Oakland, California.

MORGAN, WALLS & CLEMENTS

A newspaper article titled "Burglars at Work" detailed what transpired when a "gang of burglars" entered Octavius Morgan's home in January 1892. The reporter first complained that burglars had infested Los Angeles and robberies were a nightly occurrence in the city before he recounted Morgan's story. Morgan, whose home was at the corner of Temple and Olive Streets, was the latest victim. According to the paper, the burglars entered through a back door and found themselves in Morgan's pantry, where they stopped and took the time to drink a bottle of his wine. After they consumed the liquor, they ransacked the first floor of the house, found nothing they considered valuable and proceeded upstairs, where Morgan, his wife and two children were sleeping. The burglars entered Morgan's bedroom, scooped up his pants while he slept and went back downstairs to discover the trousers contained twenty-five dollars in one of the pockets. At this point, the burglars left and attempted to break into the house next door but were frightened away when the occupant woke up. It is hard to believe that Morgan and his family remained fast asleep while the burglars drank wine, ransacked the first floor and stumbled around the master bedroom in search of valuables. It sounds more likely that the whole family smartly played possum feigning sleep while holding their breath until the thieves vacated their home. Morgan's ability to remain silent and calm would aid him years later when he was perched on the witness stand.

OCTAVIUS MORGAN

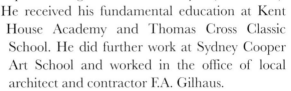

Octavius Morgan was born on October 20, 1850, in the English town of Canterbury. His parents were Giles Chapman Morgan and Caroline Tyler (née Adams). He received his fundamental education at Kent House Academy and Thomas Cross Classic School. He did further work at Sydney Cooper Art School and worked in the office of local architect and contractor F.A. Gilhaus.

After graduation, he left England and moved to the United States. In 1871, he settled in Denver, Colorado, where he obtained work in the office of an architect, contractor and builder with the last name of Nichols. In the 1870s, there was no building boom and a population of only four thousand in Denver, so work at Nichols's practice was slow. Morgan quit his job and took up the vocation of mining. Over the next three years, he would mine for gold in Colorado, Idaho, Nevada,

Octavius Morgan.
Courtesy of Greater Los Angeles & Southern California Portraits & Personal Memoranda.

Utah and Wyoming. He was unsuccessful but did not give up and eventually made his way to the state of California. In the Golden State, Morgan found enough gold in San Bernardino to make a claim, but after three years on the road, he must have been weary because he relinquished all rights to his claim and moved to Los Angeles in June 1874.

Sometime between June and December 1874, Morgan met Ezra Kysor. Kysor is the first acknowledged architect in Los Angeles and the man responsible for both the Pico House and the Merced Theater. Morgan impressed Kysor, and the two men found admirable qualities in each other; in 1875, a partnership ensued, and the firm officially changed its name to Kysor and Morgan.

Nine years later, in 1884, Morgan married Margaret Susan Weller Offenbacker, and they had two children Octavius Weller Morgan and Jessie Caroline.

JOHN A. WALLS

John A. Walls was born in Buffalo, New York, in 1860 (or 1864), and his parents were John and Hannah Walls. According to a 1930 summation of the firm Morgan, Walls & Clements published in the *Architectural Record,* Walls was educated in Buffalo and worked for several years in the architectural office of Henry Hobart Richardson. He moved to Los Angeles in 1882, and sometime after arriving, Walls went to work for Kysor and Morgan. With Kysor's retirement in 1888, the firm became Morgan and Walls. Walls married Jessie Fremont Prescott on February 9, 1892. She was from Spirit Lake, Iowa, and the couple had one daughter, Eleanor.

John A. Walls. *Courtesy of* Greater Los Angeles & Southern California Portraits & Personal Memoranda.

HOLLENBECK HOME FOR THE AGED

In 1896, the Hollenbeck Home for the Aged opened in Boyle Heights, which was an early suburb of downtown Los Angeles. Morgan and Walls designed the building in the Moorish style, and the home for the aged and the Hollenbeck mansion were situated on thirteen and a half acres in

Hollenbeck Home for the Aged depicted on a postcard. *Author's collection.*

Hollenbeck Home for the Aged staircase in main building. *Courtesy of the California History Room, California State Library, Sacramento, California.*

Hollenbeck Home for the Aged chapel. *Courtesy of the California History Room, California State Library, Sacramento, California.*

Hollenbeck Home for the Aged library. *Courtesy of the California History Room, California State Library, Sacramento, California.*

Hollenbeck Park, which contained a lake on the property and had views of the city below. Elizabeth Hollenbeck opened the home in memory of her late husband, John Edward Hollenbeck, who had died eleven years earlier. The Hollenbecks made their money in Los Angeles real estate, and the Hollenbeck Home was "a place in the city, where a forsaken, friendless, destitute woman [could] lay her head."[162]

FARMERS AND MERCHANTS NATIONAL BANK

For the Farmers and Merchants National Bank (1905), Morgan and Walls designed a two-story $400,000 Greek Revival marble-clad building on the southwest corner of Fourth and Main in downtown Los Angeles. The interior of the bank was described thus:

The splendid banking chamber is without a single column to mar the effect of the sweeping vista. In this point, the Los Angeles bank building excels many of the even costlier bank structures in eastern cities, for these as a rule, have heavy superstructures, so that the main hall in each case becomes a perfect forest of pillars. Here there is a magnificent and unbroken floor space beneath the dome of glass.[163]

Banking occupied the main floor while the basement contained the vault, lunchroom, restrooms and lockers for employees. Bank president Isaias W. Hellman directed the building to completion, and he declared the Farmers and Merchants National Bank "the finest bank structure west of Chicago."

The Farmers and Merchants Bank was declared Los Angeles Historic Cultural Monument No. 271 on August 9, 1983.

In 1909, Octavius Morgan, who was on the State Board of Architects, the organization that examined and certified architects, spoke out about licensing. Licensing was a relatively new idea at the time and had only been in place for six years. Morgan was originally nominated to the board as

Farmers and Merchants National Bank. Located at 401 South Main Street. Main Street runs along the short side. Fourth Street runs along the longer side. *Courtesy of* Western Architect.

Farmers and Merchants National Bank. Interior view from above. *Courtesy of* Western Architect.

Farmers and Merchants National Bank. Bank lobby. *Courtesy of* Western Architect.

Farmers and Merchants National Bank tellers' windows. *From an advertisement for the Winslow Brothers Company, which did ornamental iron and bronze work. The advertisement appeared in an issue of* American Architect *from 1909.*

president for the Southern California chapter in 1901, and his term was for four years, so he had served more than one term at this point. Morgan said,

> *The test is not severe, but it embodies essentials in which every man, who would properly construct a building, must be versed. The applicant for a certificate must be up on construction, design, mechanics, plumbing, electricity and a history of architecture of the past, with achievements of the present; also rendering estimates and supervision. There have been few failures since the board was placed in operation in 1903.*[164]

During these early years and into the 1920s, the law was constantly tested in court with lawsuits brought by unlicensed architects who claimed the law was invalid and by warrants against architects who practiced architecture but were unlicensed.

In May 1909, *Architect and Engineer* reported that Cass Gilbert, who was the national head of the American Institute of Architects, had appointed Morgan, who by that time was a national architectural figure, to the committee on government architecture for a one-year term. Morgan would serve on the committee with, among others, William Holabird of Chicago and Albert Pississ of San Francisco.

WALTER P. STORY BUILDING

Construction of the Walter P. Story Building, on the corner of Broadway and Sixth Streets, began in 1909. From the very beginning, it was described in news reports as a "magnificent eleven-story" building. Crowds gathered on the sidewalks fascinated by the crane that lifted long steel girders to the top of the building, and passersby strained to see the men who created all the noise via air guns and riveting hammers. In news reports, the building was compared to a mushroom. First, it was barely there, then it was three stories high and within weeks, the steel skeleton had risen to the ninth floor.[165] The public comprehended the building's immensity when it was disclosed the foundation for the W.P. Story Building began forty feet beneath street level.

Walter P. Story Building staircase. A stained-glass window is inset into the wall of the staircase, and the staircase has a skylight above too. *Courtesy of American Architect.*

All reinforced-concrete work for the retaining walls, floors and foundations was in accordance with standards set forth by the American Society of Civil Engineers. The attachment of the terra cotta and brickwork began in July. By the end of August, the brick walls and terra cotta had reached the ninth floor. The concrete floors and roof slabs were in place, and work on the plumbing and (steam) heating systems moved forward according to schedule. In November 1909, the *Herald* prematurely stated the building was "about ready for occupancy," but it would not be ready until the end of

Walter P. Story Building entrance. *Courtesy of* American Architect.

March 1910. It was then that the *Los Angeles Times* proclaimed, "Today, this imposing block stands as a superb and lasting monument to its builder and to Morgan & Walls, its architects."[166]

OCTAVIUS WELLER MORGAN (O.W.)

Octavius Weller Morgan (O.W.) the son of Octavius and Margaret Weller Morgan, was born on January 2, 1886. He was educated in Los Angeles public schools and then attended Stanford University, where he was a member of Sigma Nu. He received a degree in civil engineering in 1910, and a notice in the May 1910 issue of *Architect and Engineer* alerted the public of the firm's name change from Morgan and Walls to Morgan, Walls & Morgan.

That same year, John Walls and his wife, Jessie, and daughter, Eleanor, moved. They now lived in a large and attractive house at 2159 West Twentieth Street in Los Angeles.[167]

I.N. VAN NUYS BUILDING

On January 8, 1911, it was reported that the final papers had been signed, and construction of the I.N. Van Nuys Building, to be located at Seventh and Spring Streets, would commence in April. The Van Nuys Building was seen as "one of the most significant in the history of the city"[168] and viewed as a monument to the Van Nuys family, with no "superior" building anywhere else in the city of Los Angeles. The finished building would rank alongside the finest on the West Coast, be eleven stories tall with seven elevators and contain marble and mahogany interiors. The cost was $1.25 million, which was twice as much as any other building designed by the firm.

Isaac Newton Van Nuys bought the site in 1880 and originally used the land for his family home when the block was far from the business district. Van Nuys was a millionaire who at one timed owned forty-seven thousand acres in the San Fernando Valley. That land was sold in 1910 to the Los Angeles Suburban Homes Company, and some of the proceeds were used to erect the Van Nuys Building.

I.N. Van Nuys Building. Exterior view. *Courtesy of* American Architect.

The main tenant on the ground floor of the Van Nuys Building would be the First National Bank. The bank would also occupy the basement and have 96 feet of frontage on Seventh Street and 170 feet of frontage on Spring Street. The First National Bank took out a long lease, twenty-five years, which included an option for three extensions with the extensions running

I.N. Van Nuys Building. Staircase and lobby. *Courtesy of* American Architect.

First National Bank on the ground floor of the I.N. Van Nuys Building. *Courtesy of* American Architect.

five years each. The bank wanted to move to the southern part of the Los Angeles business district, and while some of its shareholders felt that Seventh Street might be too far south, J.M. Elliott, president of First National said,

> *7th Street is destined logically to become the great crosstown business thoroughfare of Los Angeles. We feel that the ultimate position for a bank is on a corner where not only the principal north and south movement is to be found but where the most extensive east and west traffic is eventually to be encountered as well. We do not believe we could have hit upon a better location than Seventh and Spring.*[169]

The building opened in the latter half of 1912. One newspaper article from July said the "finishing touches were being applied"[170] to the building, yet it's difficult to find a concrete date of when the building opened. It might be because I.N. Van Nuys died on February 12, 1912, and the Van Nuys family may have forgone any formal grand opening events.

The I.N. Van Nuys Building was declared Los Angeles Historic Cultural Monument No. 898 on December 5, 2007.

THE GARLAND BUILDING

Along with the Van Nuys Building, one of the first buildings the new firm of Morgan, Walls & Morgan designed was the Garland Building on Broadway, between Seventh and Eighth Streets, in Los Angeles. Announced on July 22, 1911, it was eleven stories and built for multimillionaire William Garland. The cost was $600,000, and the Garland Building not only contained offices but also a theater one hundred feet square with seating for 1,400 when the boxes, lodges, gallery and balcony were included. Plans called for the stage to be ninety feet across and thirty-eight feet deep. The Belasco was the name chosen for the theater, but the name was changed to the Morosco and eventually to the Globe. William Kerckhoff of the Pacific Light and Power Company leased several floors for twenty-one years and a total outlay, in rent, of over $1 million for the terms of the lease. Kerckhoff was a savvy man who arrived in Los Angeles in the 1880s, opened a lumberyard during one of Los Angeles' early boom periods and made a huge amount of money. He founded the Pacific Light and Power Company with some of his business friends, and the floors Kerckhoff leased in the Garland were

Garland Building. *Courtesy of* The Architect.

for the Pacific Light and Power Company. An unusual idea stressed in press reports repeatedly, regarding the Garland, was the concept of an unbroken block of skyscrapers. With the erection of the Garland Building, a missing spot was filled in on the east side of Broadway between Seventh and Eighth Streets. Even though some of the buildings in this block were only six stories high, they were still considered skyscrapers, and this block of skyscrapers was viewed as a big deal and considered by the architectural community and reporters as a major step forward for Los Angeles.

HOLLINGSWORTH BUILDING

Real estate magnate William Irving Hollingsworth announced in April 1912 that in early May, work would commence on the erection of an eleven-story office building to be called the Hollingsworth Building. The building would be located on the corner of Sixth and Hill Streets, and the firm of Morgan, Walls & Morgan had already completed the plans for the project. Hollingsworth had turned down an offer of $400,000 for the site, which faced Central Park (Pershing Square), so his estimation of the site's value (Hollingsworth worked in real estate) combined with the cost of the new building, $600,000, took the cost of the building right up to the million-dollar mark.

The Hollingsworth would have 80 feet of frontage on Hill Street and 140 feet on Sixth Street. Plans included 250 offices, with the majority overlooking Central Park. The main entrance would be on Hill Street on the south side of the building. In August 1912, Gladding-McBean received the $24,000 contract for the terra-cotta tile that would face the outside of the building.

While this building was being constructed, on November 4, 1912, the younger Morgan, O.W., married Maria Arriola, a woman born in Mexico and whose native language was Spanish. For their honeymoon, the couple went on an extended tour of the state of California by automobile. The couple eventually had four children: Octavius Weller Jr., Carlos, Perry and Robert.

The following February saw an announcement in the *Herald*, which was rare either because it happened infrequently or because, more likely, it was not normally reported. The article titled "Loses His Balance; Plunges Six Stories" recounted what happened to M.W. Harvey, who was a laborer on the Hollingsworth job site. He "plunged down the elevator shaft to the bottom and was picked up unconscious."[171] After being taken to the hospital, Harvey's injuries included a fractured skull, and his recovery was "considered doubtful." "Harvey was working alone near the elevator shaft and none of the other workmen knew of the accident until a scream ran through the building as his body started down the shaft."[172]

Harvey's fate is unclear, as no further mention of him was found in subsequent news reports.

In March 1913, the building neared completion. The terra cotta, which was described as "old ivory white," had been applied to eleven of the stories, the floors were complete and work on the interior was set to begin. The building, described as Renaissance in style, was to open on July 1, 1913. On July 12, tenants were moving into the building, and an unattributed quote in the *Herald* declared it "the masterpiece among Los Angeles' splendid office buildings."[173] A brochure produced by the Newitt Advertising Agency for prospective tenants listed various benefits to a Hollingsworth rental agreement. Some were:

- "It is just a half block off Broadway—far enough to avoid the noise and confusion of that thoroughfare—and yet Broadway practically lies in its shadow."
- "It is in close proximity to the leading men's clubs and principal hotels—and within a few steps of everything that's worth while in the downtown business district."
- "It is more than a mere architectural masterpiece—it is more than a cold, lifeless structure of steel and stone. It is the child of an ambition—a true type of a business home for the businessman as conceived and realized by a man of sentiment."[174]

THE JONQUIL "HOTEL" AFFAIR

The following events began in June 1913, and continued for over a year. It was first reported in a *Times* article with the headline "For Relief of Luckless Poor." That headline was situated under a smaller one, "Philanthropic," which had to be seen as ironic since the two subheading were "Octavius Morgan Answers the Story of Stevens" and "Frankly Tells Why He Paid Women Large Sums." What occurred first was Octavius Morgan Sr. received a visit in his office from a lawyer named W.H. Stevens who brought with him a complaint against Morgan that outlined various unsubstantiated claims. Stevens represented a young woman named Marie Brown Levy and her mother, a Mrs. Lacey.

Stevens said the girl and her mother were in an "impoverished condition"[175] and Stevens thought Morgan should do something for them. Stevens said he was sent by Charles S. McKelvey to talk to Morgan about the women's situation.

Morgan said the women's unfortunate plight so struck him that he handed Stevens a check for $1,500 and followed that up with another $1,000 check in the month of July to "put Mrs. Lacey and her daughter on their feet."[176] Morgan claimed no impropriety ever took place and said he did not even know Mrs. Lacey. Morgan said after he was given a receipt for the money, he declined to go downstairs to the lobby and meet with the mother and daughter—Stevens had brought them with him—and stated he paid these "worthy" women but he also did not want his family or the public to know he had been served with the complaint.

Morgan said he was not threatened with "exposure" by Stevens if he didn't pay but did feel he was being blackmailed. Morgan went on to say he had made the check out to Stevens and did not know if the money eventually made its way to the women.

In September 1913, Long Beach millionaire George H. Bixby was on trial for "alleged offenses against girls," and one of the girls making the accusation was Morgan's accuser Marie Brown Levy. In a *Times* article titled "Bixby's Witness Balks on Stand," Morgan tried not to answer when Bixby's lawyer asked Morgan if he knew Marie Brown Levy. Morgan, who was not on trial but had brought his own lawyer with him, objected to the question and Morgan's lawyer stated if Morgan admitted to knowing Marie Brown Levy he could open himself up to prosecution. The judge in the case excused Morgan for the day, but Bixby's lawyers said Morgan had already informed them of what had transpired between Morgan and Stevens, so Bixby's lawyers said he should be compelled to testify. Morgan, who had not yet left the court, countered by stating he viewed his conversation with Bixby's lawyers as confidential.

The judge saw it differently. Morgan again took the stand, but as he dodged the prosecutor's questions, a disturbance outside of the courtroom became obvious to everyone inside. It originated in the witness room and was caused by Mrs. Lacey. It began with loud sobs, but when officers entered the holding area of the witness room, Mrs. Lacey caused such a hysterical commotion it was deemed necessary to take her to a local hospital. Once she was escorted away and had left the building, it was her daughter's turn. The Levy girl's behavior was not as dramatic as her mother's so she was allowed to calm herself and remain in the waiting area. Some of Octavius Morgan's testimony at the Bixby trial was printed in the *San Francisco Call*. It was a short excerpt, but it showed how reluctant he was to testify and how little he said even when he answered. It consisted of:

Q: "Do you know attorney W. H. Stevens?"
Morgan: "I object."
Judge: "Answer."
Morgan: "Yes, I know him."
Q: "Did you see him during the past summer?"
Morgan: "Yes."
Q: "Did you ever give him a check?"
Morgan's attorney (Weaton A Gray): "I think the witness ought to be excused from answering that question. If he answers that question it will be inferred that he submitted to blackmail, and much more of a degrading nature will be inferred."[177]

The same article that featured the printed testimony contained an admonishment from the judge overseeing the case who stated he would ask the bar to investigate Stevens and McKelvey. His words were, "These men must be either vindicated of the inference that they did the actual work of extorting money from Morgan or they must be punished."[178]

The judge got his wish. In October 1914, all of Morgan's interactions with Stevens were revealed, as Morgan was then a government witness against Stevens and McKelvey in a U.S. District Court. The two lawyers were charged with "using the mails for blackmailing purposes."

Stevens and McKelvey were eventually convicted, fined and disbarred. Stevens was jailed too. The court showed some leniency with McKelvey because he was fifty-five and had been practicing law in Southern California for over twenty-five years. One final and important item of note is, often, whenever the various newspapers reporting on the trial mentioned Marie Brown Levy or Mrs. Lacey, the women's address was given as the Jonquil apartments or Jonquil "Hotel," and the word *hotel* was often in quotation marks. This was deliberate. Local newspapers were letting their readers know the Jonquil was an establishment with a questionable reputation. In one article, Morgan stated the only reason he went to the Jonquil was because one of the ladies who lived at the establishment wanted to know if any of his associates had any vacant apartments. Other men who were called to testify at Stevens and McKelvey's trial used fake names when checking into the Jonquil. One man, Kyle MacBratney of El Centro, not only admitted to using an alias when checking into the Jonquil but also confessed that the woman with him at the time of his check-in—whom he claimed was his wife then—was not his wife.

After the trial, Morgan spent a great deal of time away from Los Angeles traveling. The whole Marie Brown Levy affair did not seem to hurt his business, but Morgan had to have been embarrassed by the whole situation. Morgan was never charged with any offense, was subjected to blackmail and paid the blackmail but claimed he did so only to keep the unsubstantiated charges out of the public sphere. Since the claims were never revealed in press reports, Angelinos following the story were left to imagine what they were.

HAAS BUILDING

In the mid-1910s, Morgan, Walls & Morgan erected the Haas Building at the corner of Seventh and Broadway. The Haas Building (1915) was heralded with the newspaper headline "Marble Lined Palace of Future Business." Millionaire Abraham Haas, who was president of Haas-Baruch & Company, had extensive real estate holdings in Los Angeles and this corner at Seventh and Broadway was his prime location. The Haas office block was to contain 225 offices on the upper floors with interior finishes

Haas (*left*) and Hollingsworth (*right*) Buildings. *Courtesy of* The Architect.

that included solid mahogany, marble floors and marble wainscoting that went up the walls seven feet. The exterior of the building was to be clad in white terra cotta. The Bank of Italy signed a twenty-five-year lease for the ground-floor space.

KERCKHOFF BUILDING

Because of the financial depression of 1914, construction was delayed for two years, but work finally began on the new Kerckhoff Building in the last week of November 1915 according to the *Times*. Yet the *Los Angeles Herald* reported that the building's permit was issued on January 8, 1916. This new Kerckhoff Building was located on the northwest corner of Sixth and Los Angeles Streets. The *Times* stated the building was constructed of reinforced concrete, was eight stories high and cost approximately $500,000. The *Herald* contradicted the *Times* and said the cost was $325,000. When it was finished, the Santa Fe Railroad occupied the top seven floors of the building while a variety of shops leased the first floor. Alaskan marble covered the first floor's entrance and lobby, and all interior woodwork was either mahogany or birch. Granite covered the exterior of the first floor, and the other seven stories had an ivory-enameled brick covering with terra-cotta trimmings.

The Kerckhoff Building and Annex were declared Los Angeles Historic Cultural Monument No. 806 on June 1, 2005.

O.W. Morgan registered for the draft on September 12, 1918. His draft registration card stated he had brown eyes, dark hair and a medium build. During World War I, O.W. was a first lieutenant of engineers, and when discharged, he was a captain of engineers.

THE YEAR 1922

While 1913 and 1914 may have been difficult years for the firm, the year 1922 was worse.

Ten years after O.W. and Maria were married, in January 1922, a *Los Angeles Times* article appeared with the headline "Says Architect Cruel to Wife." Its sub-headline was "Mrs. O.W. Morgan Files Suit for Legal

Odd Fellows Temple near the corner of Second and Main Streets. *Courtesy* of Los Angeles of Today Architecturally.

Separation." Those two headlines were not the most sensational. The sensational ones were "Letters from Other Woman Cited in Complaint" and "Lavished Money on Rivals, Is Her Charge."

In the article, Maria Morgan claimed her marital trouble began after O.W. returned from the war. The first clue that something was amiss was when a postcard, from another woman, fell from the pocket of his army uniform. She then discovered a letter from the same woman that was "couched in endearing terms."[179] Maria then claimed O.W. was making frequent trips to Catalina Island, and she suspected unidentified women were with him. Maria's complaint stated O.W. was often seen in the city's "exclusive cafes" with women and he spent lavishly on them. O.W. Morgan was making about $1,000 a month in 1922, and Maria claimed that a large portion of that money was being spent on these unidentified women. Her lawyers were Janeway, Beach and Pratt, and Maria was requesting $750 a month in alimony and custody of the couple's children.

Two months later, on March 29, 1922, after a day that involved attending a meeting of the Allied Architects and a night at the theater, Octavius

Morgan died from "heart disease" at the age of seventy-two. Morgan was a member of the Jonathan Club, a Mason and a member of the Odd Fellows' fraternity. He also was the first president of the State Board of Architects, a former president of the American Institute of Architects Southern California chapter and a former president of the Architects and Engineers Association. Morgan is buried at the Inglewood Park Cemetery. His wife, Margaret, and two children, O.W. and Jessie Caroline, were his survivors.

Nine months later, on December 12, 1922, John A. Walls died. Walls was an enigma. He stayed out of trouble and, fortunately for his wife, never had his name splashed across a newspaper's headline in an unsavory or lurid way. He was so under the radar that there was no obituary for him in either the *Los Angeles Times* or the *Los Angeles Herald*. He is buried in the Great Mausoleum at Forest Lawn Memorial Park in Glendale, California. He was survived by his wife, Jessie, and daughter, Eleanor.

During their partnership, Morgan and Walls also designed in downtown Los Angeles the Odd Fellows Temple at Second and Main Street (1895), the Van Nuys Hotel (1897) and the first Pantages Theater on Broadway (1910).

STILES O. CLEMENTS

The firm of Morgan, Walls & Clements wouldn't have the reputation it has today if it wasn't for Stiles Oliver Clements. After the deaths of Octavius Morgan Sr. and John A. Walls in 1922, "in 1923 the firm was reorganized under the name of Morgan, Walls & Clements."[180] Paired with O.W. Morgan, the firm retained Walls's name even though Walls was deceased. From Centerville, Maryland, Clements was born on March 2, 1883. His father was a doctor named Thomas, and his mother's name was Mary. Stiles also had a much younger brother named Thomas born in 1896. Stiles moved to Los Angeles in 1911. Architectural historian David Gebhard wrote that the reason Morgan, Walls &

Stiles O. Clements, circa 1948. *Courtesy of © J. Paul Getty Trust. Getty Research Institute, Los Angeles (2004.R.10).*

Morgan hired Clements was because the partners felt their architectural style was too tied to the past and they needed someone with a new outlook on design. Clements, who was a graduate of Drexel and MIT, went off to the École des Beaux-Arts in Paris for a year after graduation. Walls and both Morgans were probably impressed with his résumé.

Clements married Ida McAvoy on February 15, 1917, and they had four children—Robert, Mary, Harold and Margaret.

ODD FELLOWS TEMPLE

In August 1922, the Odd Fellows announced the organization had engaged Morgan, Walls & Morgan to construct an Odd Fellows Temple at the corner of Twelfth and Flower Streets. This land, on the northwest corner, had been acquired more than a decade before for the sole purpose of building a temple on the site. The temple would be three stories, have six lodge rooms on the second and third floors and have one hundred feet of frontage on the Flower Street side. There would be a banquet room and a smoking room in the basement along with the mechanical systems. The title for the building would be held by the Odd Fellows Temple Company, which comprised all six downtown lodges, with the cost of the building being $250,000.

There is no evidence this building was ever erected.

On June 20, 1925, an Odd Fellows Temple was instead dedicated at the corner of Washington Boulevard and Oak Street, approximately one mile from the Flower and Twelfth Streets location. Morgan, Walls & Clements were the architects for this building. This temple had five lodge rooms, three ballrooms and five retail stores facing Washington Street. Five downtown lodges took part in the development and construction. Those lodges were America, Golden Rule, Goodwill, Los Angeles and Semi-Tropic. The temple's final cost was $500,000. The men who oversaw the dedication were the state grand master, the deputy grand master and the acting grand chaplain. Activities on the dedication day included tours, a ball in honor of the temple's completion and the visitation of state Odd Fellow officers along with a parade that started at the corner of Pico and Figueroa and included 125 members of the local canton and the Santa Monica Odd Fellows Band.

A September 1925 article in *California Southland* mentioned O.W. Morgan and his ranch in the Glendora (California) area. In a few sentences, it brought

Odd Fellows Temple at Washington and Oak Streets in Los Angeles. *Courtesy of* Architectural Digest Southern California *commercial edition.*

to light a different type of existence for O.W, surrounded by men who saw him as an equal, with drinks and food. The article detailed the August meeting of the Southern California chapter of the American Institute of Architects, which was held at Morgan's ranch. The event's guest speaker that evening was the Southwest Museum's Charles Lummis, who spoke about the restoration of the Santa Barbara mission.

Eight years after her complaint, as the 1920s turned into the 1930s, Morgan divorced his first wife, Maria, and married Selma H. Krueger. In 1929, Morgan was forty-four, and he would tell census workers in 1930 his marriage to Krueger was his first marriage, so his marriage to Maria was completely erased from his memory.

RICHFIELD OIL BUILDING

One of the greatest art deco buildings ever built in Los Angeles was torn down over a two-year period from 1968 to 1969. It was the Richfield Oil Building, and it was built in 1928–29 by Morgan, Walls & Clements. The Richfield Oil Building was replaced by ARCO plaza, which contains two international-style skyscrapers.

Architectural historian David Gebhard wrote a twenty-eight-page book on the building titled *The Richfield Building*, produced and published by Atlantic Richfield right after the building was demolished. Gebhard accurately compared the Richfield Building to Raymond Hood's American Radiator Building in New York City; not only were they vertical buildings similarly

Left: Richfield Oil Building viewed from the park across the street. *Courtesy of the California History Room, California State Library, Sacramento, California.*

Right: Richfield Oil Building angels were sold for $100 each when the building was demolished. *Courtesy of* California Arts and Architecture *February 1930.*

clad in black and gold but both faced parks so they could be seen from a distance and close-up via the sidewalk as well.

He also endorsed Esther McCoy's theory that the Richfield Building is a combination of both high art and low art. The high art being the newness of the design—art deco was only five years old in 1930. The Paris Exposition des Arts Décoratifs took place in 1925. The low art aspect was sticking a large, neon sign on top of the building to sell Richfield Oil.

Haig Patigian, the sculptor of the angel figures on the building, was well known in his time. He was Armenian, born in 1876, self-trained and twice president of the Bohemian Club in San Francisco. His sculpture was seen at the Panama-Pacific Exposition, and he modeled figures for that exhibition's Palace of Machinery Hall, which was designed by the architectural firm of Ward & Blohme. He also designed the figures in the pediment of the Metropolitan Life Insurance Building in San Francisco and was a member of the National Sculptor Society. When the Richfield Building was demolished, the angels were removed and sold for $100 each. Two of the angels were decapitated during the removal process and some lost their wings.

Left: Richfield Oil Building entrance. *Courtesy of the California History Room, California State Library, Sacramento, California.*

Right: Richfield Oil Building at night. *Courtesy of the California History Room, California State Library, Sacramento, California.*

Opposite: Richfield Oil Building entrance figures. A total of four figures stood above the entrance portal to the Richfield Building. Three of these figures were relocated to the UC Santa Barbara campus. *Courtesy of* Architect and Engineer.

In *California Arts and Architecture*, Harris Allen makes an interesting evaluation of the building that only someone who had seen it could make. Allen described the terra cotta in particular:

> *They* [the bricks] *are not really black. The building in New York* [The American Radiator Building] *which first displayed a color scheme of black and gold, was faced with a dull black brick, and the gold was contained to the top of the tower. It is certainly less theatrical, more integral to weave the colors together in a more structural way and the black is more of a gun-metal shade, in some lights bluish or purplish gray.*[181]

Allen pointed out something else that may have escaped people regarding this building. Allen said the reason the colors are black and gold is because oil is often referred to as black gold. Oil = black gold, hence the colors.

Architect Robert Harris said when an architect approaches a new project he should understand "what already exists—that is of great value and quality—[and] should not be damaged." Harris's fundamental edict was repeatedly ignored in the 1960s, which was, ironically, the decade that saw the creation of the National Trust for Historic Preservation in the United States. The 1960s were a terrible time for great buildings. In that decade alone, the Richfield Building was demolished along with Pennsylvania Station in New York City, the Imperial Hotel in Tokyo, the Fox movie theater in San Francisco, both the Roxy Theater and Astor Hotel in New York and practically all of downtown Minneapolis. If these buildings had held on for another ten or fifteen years, they would have survived that precarious decade and probably would still be with us today. Urban renewal was the culprit and the scourge of the twentieth century.

In David Gebhard's book, he has a short paragraph near the end in which he doesn't even mourn the building's passing. He simply states more office space was needed so the building was brought down. Since the book was published by Atlantic Richfield, I suspect he couldn't say much more, but how glorious it would be today to walk through the Richfield Building's entrance portal and marvel at the architectural expertise of Morgan, Walls & Clements.

SAMSON TIRE AND RUBBER COMPANY

One of Morgan, Walls & Clements most spectacular buildings began construction in 1929 in the city of Commerce. It's the Samson Tire and Rubber Company building.

The man who commissioned the building was Adolph Schleicher. He was both founder and president of Samson Tire. In the 1920s, Los Angeles was a city still finding itself architecturally. It was a hodgepodge of styles. This explains how an Egyptian theater and a Chinese theater ended up blocks apart and probably explains how Southern California ended up with an Assyrian wall next to a freeway.

Samson Tire and Rubber is located at 5675 Telegraph Road in the city of Commerce and "it's a 1,700-foot-long Assyrian wall and facade, a replica of a palace for King Sargon II found during excavation of the ancient city of Khorsabad in present day Iraq,"[182] according to a newspaper report.

Above: Samson Tire and Rubber Building is now known as the Citadel Outlet Mall. It is located at 100 Citadel Drive in the city of Commerce. *Author photo.*

Right: Samson Tire and Rubber Building. Incised decoration on one section of the wall. *Author photo.*

The groundbreaking ceremony took place on January 23, 1929, but first there was a 5.5-mile parade that started at the corner of Ninth Street and Boyle Avenue. The parade route was marked by flags and included the participation of several east-side bands and 250 cars. A festive note occurred regularly during the parade when it was confetti-bombed by airplanes that flew over the parade route. At the actual groundbreaking ceremony, chamber of commerce president Shannon Crandall proclaimed that henceforth the Akron of the West would be Los Angeles.[183] Mayor Cryer also addressed the assembled crowd, and Schleicher's two daughters Gretchen and Nancy Ellen used a silver pick and a silver spade to turn the first mounds of earth.

When the tire company went out of business in 1978, after almost fifty years on the site, the city took control of the building and eventually purchased it in 1983 for $14 million. What emerged from a competition held to refurbish the building and the surrounding land was the Citadel Outlet Mall. So, eighty-eight years after it was built, this mammoth Assyrian wall, which looks like it is a set piece from D.W. Griffith's film *Intolerance*, stands

Samson Tire and Rubber Building. One of the Assyrian griffins that flank the entrance. *Author photo.*

Samson Tire and Rubber Building entrance. Most people park behind the building and enter from the rear, but the front doors are unlocked during business hours. *Author photo.*

beside the freeway as a signpost to motorists as they zoom past unfazed by its existence.

During the 1920s and 1930s, the firm of Morgan, Walls & Clements designed in Hollywood the El Capitan Theater (1926), the Music Box Theater (1926), the Hollywood Box Corporation (1929), the Hollywood Chamber of Commerce (1929), the Pig'n Whistle (1930) and the Julian Medical Building (1933). In Los Angeles, it designed the Bank of Italy (1923), the Belasco Theater (1926), the Mayan Theater (1927), the Chouinard School of Art (1930), the Dominguez-Wilshire Building (1930), the Pellissier Building (1931) and the Leimert Theater (1931).[184]

STILES AND O.W.

Clements was instrumental in the design of all of the firm's major buildings in the 1920s and 1930s. Clements left Morgan, Walls & Clements in 1937 to form his own architectural firm, which he called Stiles O. Clements and Associates.

O.W. Morgan lived for another fourteen years after Clements's departure before he died suddenly on May 17, 1951. He is buried beside his father and the rest of his family in Inglewood, California. He was survived by his wife, Selma, four sons and his sister, Mrs. Jessie M. McGilvray. O.W. was a member of the American Institute of Architects, Flintridge Country Club, Los Angeles Country Club, Los Angles Athletic Club, Jonathan Club, University Club, Al Malaikah Temple of the Shrine, Scottish Rite and the Recreation Gun Club. He also was a member of the Los Angeles traffic commission in 1926.

In the 1940s and 1950s, Stiles O. Clements' firm designed over fifty buildings on Wilshire Boulevard alone, including the Carnation Building and Mullen-Bluett Building. It was one of the biggest firms in Los Angeles in the postwar years. The firm did mid-century modern–style Sears stores along with mid-century modern Vons and Ralphs grocery stores all over the southland from Pasadena to Pomona. One of Clements's sons, Robert, became a partner in his father's firm in 1955, and the company's name was changed that year to Stiles & Robert Clements Architects-Engineers.[185] The other son, Harold McAvoy Clements, also was an architect but his name wasn't attached prominently to the firm probably because he was charged with manslaughter in 1954. In an auto accident, a pregnant woman was ejected

Stiles O. Clements's office door, circa 1948. *Courtesy of © J. Paul Getty Trust. Getty Research Institute, Los Angeles (2004.R.10).*

from one of the other vehicles involved, and Harold Clements ran over her, which resulted in the death of the woman and her unborn child. Harold Clements was found not guilty of manslaughter.[186]

One of the firm's most interesting commissions involved a building it never built. The Clements firm was selected, in 1949, to design the Los Angeles Sports Arena in Exposition Park. The undertaking was a long process hindered by layers of governmental input, but the Clements firm finally submitted plans and was awaiting its initial payment of $150,000 when the Los Angeles Coliseum Commission suddenly rejected the plans. The Coliseum Commission claimed the plans were created in a careless and unprofessional manner that caused the cost of the sports arena to skyrocket.[187] The Clements firm sued for $346,000 in lost profits, and the Coliseum Commission countersued for $365,667. In 1957, the commission decided that the Clements firm breached the contract and ended the relationship. New firms considered for the job included Albert C. Martin & Associates, Pereira & Luckman and Welton Becket & Associates.[188] Welton Becket & Associates received the commission, and that sports arena was sadly demolished in 2016.

Stiles O. Clements continued to work into the 1960s. He retired in 1965 and retreated to his Beverly Hills home of thirty-one years. He died at Good Samaritan Hospital on January 15, 1966. He was eighty-two years old. His wife died in 1960. His survivors included his two sons, Robert and Harold, and two daughters, Margaret and Mary, along with numerous grandchildren. He is buried at Forest Lawn Memorial Park in Glendale, California.

KYSOR AND MORGAN

Ezra Kysor retired from the firm of Kysor and Morgan in 1888 to work in real estate, the buying and selling of land and property. In subsequent years, the majority of Kysor's architectural work was destroyed simply because the city evolved, but Morgan, in collaboration with a series of partners, created a firm that at one time was responsible for one-third of the architectural work done in Los Angeles. Most of Morgan, Walls & Clements' best buildings have survived and still grace the streets of Los Angeles. As the firm evolved from the 1870s to the 1930s, the buildings went from contained and reserved to flashy and soaring. The I.N. Van Nuys Building of 1912 is understated when it's compared to the Richfield Building of 1930. Likewise, the Octavius Morgan who played possum during a home break-in in 1892 is not the same man who appeared in the pages of the press in 1914. Morgan had gone from a timid family man hiding under the blankets, to someone carelessly risking everything at the Jonquil "Hotel." People make mistakes all the time, but what Octavius Morgan got right and what he accomplished can be seen every day by Angelinos and tourists traversing the overcrowded streets of Southern California and looking up at the constructed landscape.

The California State Board of Examiners, the organization that oversees the licensing of architects, gives out a special award every year called the Octavius Morgan Distinguished Service Award. It is appropriate and just that the man responsible for so much of the built environment in Southern California is remembered and honored by an organization that continues the work he began at the turn of the twentieth century.

ALFRED F. ROSENHEIM

A lfred Faist Rosenheim was eighty years old, in 1939, when he spoke
disparagingly about modernism and the design of his latest building,
the Hollenbeck Jr. High School.
Rosenheim said,

*Personally, I do not hesitate to express the fervent hope that "modernistic"
architecture is not a permanent trend. I have a strong feeling that the bulk
of modern work we see the country over has very little claim to architectural
beauty. In fact I am inclined to doubt whether it can strictly be regarded as
architecture…but, whatever one chooses to call the style of my Hollenbeck
School, it seemed to appeal to the Board of Education.*[189]

Rosenheim was born in St. Louis on June 10, 1859. Of German heritage,
he attended public schools in St. Louis; at the age of thirteen, Rosenheim
was sent to Germany to attend the Hassel's Institute. He returned to
America two years later and, from 1874 to 1879, attended St. Louis's
Washington University, followed by a stint at MIT from 1879 to 1881. He
did not graduate from MIT. Rosenheim married Frances Graham Wheelock
in 1884 and then stumbled onto some luck by gaining employment in the
office of Major Francis D. Lee, who was a prominent St. Louis architect. Lee
died the following year, but Rosenheim was able to charm his way through
the St. Louis architectural community and worked for a variety of firms over
the next fifteen years. In the same article in which he criticized modernism,

Left: Alfred F. Rosenheim at the height of his success. *Courtesy of* Architectural Record.

Right: Alfred Rosenheim bookplate. *Author's collection.*

Rosenheim remembered with pride his first substantial commission as an architect in St. Louis and how that building was better built than the law required. His work in St. Louis caught the eye of Herman W. Hellman, who was looking to build a monument to himself, and it was Hellman who lured Rosenheim to Los Angeles.

THE HELLMAN BUILDING

In August 1902, newspapers announced that Herman W. Hellman had plans to erect a building at the corner of Fourth and Spring Streets, and it was slated to be the biggest building ever undertaken in Los Angeles. One newspaper compared the proposed Hellman Building to the Call Building in San Francisco and stated that while it wouldn't be as tall as the Call Building, it would "have certain modern features that had not been put into successful operation when that structure was designed."[190] The architect of the building, newspapers announced, was Alfred F. Rosenheim, a transplant to the city from St. Louis.

Herman Hellman Building on a postcard. *Author's collection.*

Herman Hellman Building interior.
Author photo.

The Hellman Building was officially scheduled to be eight stories tall, but if the basement and attic were added into the mix, it would be unofficially ten stories. It was designed to be a steel-framed building and absolutely fireproof. The Fourth Street entrance was to be 24 feet wide and the building's frontage along the street was 190 feet. The Spring Street entrance was 17 feet wide with 118 feet of frontage. Where the hallways from both entrances intersected, four high-speed electric elevators "designed to travel at the rate of 500 feet a minute" were slated to be installed.

The exterior of the building would be clad in two different materials, granite on the first two floors and the sill course of the third story. Bly Brothers Stone Company, which had a quarry near Riverside, was the granite supplier, and the estimated cost of the granite was $50,000. Above the sill course, also known as an ornamental cornice, would be granite-colored hydraulic-pressed brick supplied by the Simmons Brick company at a cost of $15,000.

A twelve-foot-deep basement and a twenty-four-foot deep subbasement were part of the design scheme along with 270 offices on the upper seven floors, and all were to be heated and "ventilated" in the vein of modern buildings in Chicago and New York. Monthly rents would range from twenty-five to fifty dollars depending on their size and floor location.

Two notable features were mentioned in news reports. The first was a large director's room that would be available to Hellman tenants, if needed, along with a free law library.

The building was designed in the Beaux-Arts style with a white marble lobby and a central dome illuminated by sunlight. Originally slated to cost $750,000, the final price tag was closer to $1 million; some sources claim the final cost was $1.5 million.[191]

The Hellman Building was declared Los Angeles Historic Cultural Monument No. 729 on October 18, 2002.

MISAPPROPRIATION OF FUNDS

In July 1904, Rosenheim was dragged into court, along with his wife, Frances, by William H. Leonard, who accused both of misappropriation of funds. Their victim, according to Leonard, was an elderly woman named Harriet M. Arnold, who had recently died. Leonard was Arnold's nephew, and Frances Rosenheim was Arnold's niece, making William H. Leonard and Frances Rosenheim cousins. The Rosenheims were accused of taking $100,000 in funds from Arnold. The court case involved two wills. The Rosenheims had a will dated April 1902, while Charles W. Buker, William H. Leonard and C.A. Scott possessed a will dated April 1903.

Newspaper accounts summarized the court case this way: Rosenheim had power of attorney for Arnold and was accused of appropriating stocks and dividends that belonged to Arnold for his own use. Rosenheim was said to have in his possession 3,100 shares in the Pratt Mercantile company valued at $57,745.74 and another group of shares (300) valued at $42,000 that had been purchased with Arnold's money and held by Rosenheim.

Leonard, after a protracted visit with Arnold that lasted from February to May 1903, convinced her that Rosenheim was "crooked" and urged her to write a new will that did not list the Rosenheim family as beneficiaries. Once Arnold died, the battle of the two wills went on for three years. It was finally resolved in January 1907, with Charles W. Buker designated the executor of the estate. Newspapers didn't cover the details concerning the final resolution in probate court, but the fact that Buker, who was Leonard's ally, was made executor indicates this wasn't a victory for Rosenheim.

Rosenheim had a great deal to lose over the court case, and the negative publicity hanging over his head couldn't have been good for his reputation. It's possible that after the protracted battle the two sides came to an agreement whereby Rosenheim simply returned the shares of Pratt Mercantile to the estate so the probate of the will could take place.

SUCCESS AND FAILURE

In 1905, Rosenheim received the contract to erect a huge building for the Hamburger Department Store. It was to be the downtown flagship store. The project proceeded smoothly for approximately two years, and then it didn't. A problem occurred while the building was being erected that resulted in Rosenheim's removal from the project. It is unclear what happened. In his book *Homage to Downtown*, Jim Crandell wrote,

> *It cannot, as yet, be ascertained exactly why Rosenheim was fired by the Hamburgers approximately two years later. Press accounts revealed that he had entered into questionable financial arrangements with the project. [A.C.] Martin's sons gave varying accounts; one related technical problems arose during the building's construction. The other son claimed that Rosenheim, who was related to the Hamburgers, had been involved in an adulterous adventure and was immediately let go by the retailers.*[192]

Whatever the reason, Rosenheim is still the acknowledged architect of the building. In spite of this professional setback, Rosenheim was elected president of the Southern California chapter of the American Institute of Architects in 1906 and 1907. Rosenheim was one of the key members of the organization, and he served on numerous AIA committees, including schoolhouse plans, entertainment, competitions, press and uniform office

Hamburger Department Store. *Courtesy of* Architect and Engineer.

rules. He was often asked to contact city officials about matters that concerned the Southern California chapter and was instrumental in writing condolence letters to grieving relatives, as was the case with Max Jenny, William Lebaron Jenny's son, when Jenny died in Los Angeles in 1907. Yet what Rosenheim probably did best was mentioned in the AIA minutes of one meeting in 1906. It said the Southern California chapter held a dinner for the State Board of Architecture staff and Rosenheim "acted as toastmaster."

Through the years, in various journals and newspapers, it was frequently reported that Rosenheim was the master of ceremonies at a proceeding or the host at a banquet or was described raising his glass before making a toast or being congratulated on his captivating personality. From what is recounted in the AIA minutes, it sounds as if

Advertisement for the 1913 architectural exhibit held at the Hamburger Department Store. *From the* Year Book: Los Angeles Architectural Club, *1913.*

he was a good storyteller too. Even after being let go from the Hamburger project, he was back at the Hamburger's department store "acting as toastmaster" for an architectural exhibit held at the venue a few years later.

Rosenheim, by all accounts, was a very charming man.

In 1907, Rosenheim built a large and attractive house on Westchester Place, which was a new subdivision in Los Angeles. The home had 200 feet of frontage, and the lot was 150 feet deep. Constructed of stone and brick, it was terraced and had elaborate landscaped lawns. The Rosenheims employed two servants and a cook, but since the home had a mortgage, the Rosenheims also had two male boarders living with them, an architect named Williams S. Eames from St. Louis and a draftsman named Clinton A. Frothingham.

In 1908, Rosenheim wrote an article for *Architect and Engineer* regarding steel construction. He did so because he was always being accused of being "an out and out steel man."

He wrote:

> *I believe it would be perfectly safe to venture the statement that we are practically all agreed that well designed steel construction, properly protected*

and fire-proofed, for whatever purpose it may be utilized, is superior to any other method of construction that has been yet devised and that it is the safest method because the calculation of stresses, strains, loads, etc., has been reduced to an exact scientific basis. On the other hand, I seriously doubt whether a similar assertion can be made with respect to reinforced concrete construction.[193]

CLUNE'S BROADWAY THEATER

The estimated cost to build the Clune's Broadway Theater, which still stands today, was $50,000. That was in 1910, and that estimate included all the furnishings. The building is situated on a 60-foot-by-160-foot lot at 526 Broadway and includes two exits, behind the screen, which can funnel theatergoers into the adjacent alley behind the theater in case of an emergency.

The lobby was decorated in marble and stucco and had a vaulted ceiling and a simple steel marquee. This was before the huge lighted marquee that became standard in the 1920s and 1930s with the emergence of picture palaces.

The auditorium had a large skylight over the seating area, but there was no balcony and no boxes attached to any of the side walls. The total seating capacity for the theater was nine hundred.

Clunes Broadway Theater was declared Los Angeles Cultural Historic Monument No. 524 on March 20, 1991.

SECOND CHURCH OF CHRIST, SCIENTIST

The dome of the Second Church of Christ, Scientist is what sparked the interest of most architects and engineers when the building was announced in 1905. The dome was of particular interest because of the steel framework and how the steel did away with "the necessity of heavy shoring and bracing,"[194] which is almost always essential in concrete construction. The four concrete trusses that supported the dome could carry 350 tons and were considered one of the most important architectural features of the church. The spans of the trusses were sixty-eight feet long and had twenty-foot depths at the supports. The concrete dome was the largest ever constructed.

Albert C. Martin, who would go on to carve out a name for himself in the Los Angeles landscape, was the engineer on the project, and his name often appeared alongside Rosenheim's when the project was mentioned.

This building was hailed at the time as the "most elaborate" church going up west of Chicago. Its style was declared by *Concrete and Engineering* magazine as Roman Corinthian, but H.M. Finley of the *Los Angeles Times* said it was Italian Renaissance. Mahogany wood was used for the wainscoting, pews, doors and other interior wood detailing. The floor was designed with interlocking rubber tile.

One of the dictates of the Christian Science Church specifies that a church cannot be dedicated till all debt related to its construction has been paid off, but that doesn't mean the doors of the church couldn't be opened to the public beforehand. On January 23, 1910, the Christian Science church located at 948 West Adams opened its door to the public with four scheduled services: 9:00 a.m., 11:00 a.m., 3:00 p.m. and 8:00 p.m. Even though the church's auditorium had a seating capacity of 1,200, the four services failed to accommodate all the people who showed up to attend opening day services.

Newspaper accounts state that long before the services began, in some cases hours before, the auditorium was filled to capacity, the doors were

Second Church of Christ, Scientist. *Courtesy of* The Brickbuilder.

Second Church of
Christ, Scientist.
Author photo.

Second Church of Christ, Scientist. Interior photo looking toward rostrum. *Courtesy of* The Brickbuilder.

closed and individuals who traveled great distances were turned away. For its opening day, and in all Christian Science churches around the world, the word of the day was Truth. Local readers during the service were S. Manson Abbott and Nancy T. Craig.

The lot the church stands upon runs 200 feet across Adams Boulevard and is 250 feet deep. The church sits in the center of the plot and is 100 feet by 150 feet. The land was purchased in 1905 for $20,000, and once that cost was paid off, the construction of the church began. The final cost of the church was $300,000.

The church was declared Los Angeles Historic Cultural Monument No. 57 in August 1968.

OUTWARD APPEARANCES

Rosenheim was elected the president of the Architectural League of the Pacific Coast in 1910. That same year, Rosenheim was elected president of the Engineers and Architects Association. Rosenheim attended the AIA annual convention in 1911 and reported back to the Southern California chapter "with an extensive and interesting account of the proceedings of the Convention which was received with considerable applause by the Chapter members present."[195] Rosenheim was also elected to the American Institute of Architects' national board of directors for three years, in 1911, 1912 and 1913. In 1914, Rosenheim's home was burglarized. The thieves entered through a window, and according to Rosenheim, the burglars made off with numerous stickpins engraved with Rosenheim's initials and set with diamonds and rubies.

Despite the outward appearance of being a highly successful architect, in June 1916, Rosenheim filed for bankruptcy in the U.S. district court. It must have been embarrassing. William Randolph Hearst's *Los Angeles Herald* didn't allow the bankruptcy to go quietly unnoticed; instead, it ran an article on Rosenheim titled "L.A. Architect Asks to Be Declared Bankrupt." The short news item allowed the citizens of Los Angeles to read about Rosenheim's financial problems for the cost of a one-cent paper.

In need of cash, two years later, Rosenheim sold the house on Westchester Place to A.J. McQuatters, a mining man from El Paso. In 1918, Rosenheim was working in Washington, D.C., as a structural engineer for the government, but by 1920, he had returned to Los Angeles and was renting a house on West

Pico. Once again, Alfred and Frances Rosenheim had boarders. This time, two female boarders. One was Ruth R. Salmons, and the other was Mary A. Moore. Frances's brother, Benjamin Wheelock, also lived with them.

THE MUNICIPAL ART COMMISSION

Rosenheim ran into some trouble while working as a commissioner for the Municipal Art Commission in 1921. In February of that year, Rosenheim was accused of taking a $250 fee for a matter that was pending before the Municipal Art Commission. According to section 18 of the Los Angeles city charter, that was prohibited; city officials could not participate financially in any transaction pending before them in their official capacity. The city charter allowed for prosecution of the offender, and if the official was found guilty, the official could be removed from office.

The details of the incident were as follows: The Italian Jewelry Company of 205 North Spring Street applied on January 26, 1921, to erect a large ornamental clock on the sidewalk in front of its store. Plans were drawn up and submitted to the Municipal Art Commission on February 1. The Municipal Art Commission rejected the plans. Ray E. Lundy, who represented the Italian Jewelry Company, then sought out Rosenheim, at his office, and after a brief conversation Rosenheim said he would "look after the matter for you if you desire."[196] Lundy agreed, and the next day a letter arrived at the Italian Jewelry Company addressed to Arturo de Caro, the owner of the jewelry store. The letter said:

Dear Sir: In regard to the sidewalk clock you desired to have erected in front of your store and which Mr. Lundy talked to me about this morning, beg to advise you that I will be pleased to render the service necessary to produce a first-class structure for a net fee of $250.00 of which I shall expect $100 to be paid in advance. This service will include the preparation of the preliminary sketches and studies, the general and detailed drawings and specifications, inviting bids from responsible concerns, letting the contract and supervising the actual construction of the work in the shop, and its erection in position in front of your store. I can safely guarantee to make a design that will meet with the approval of the Municipal Art Commission as required. However, in order to do this in time for submission to the commission at its meeting to be held Wednesday forenoon next at 11 o'clock *means rush work and temporarily setting aside other important work on which I am engaged. If this is satisfactory to you, I will proceed to study the problem promptly on receipt of your check for $100 and endeavor to have the sketch ready for the meeting referred to. Awaiting your commands, I am, very truly yours, A.F. Rosenheim.*[197]

Lundy and De Caro "saw the light" according to newspaper accounts and sent a check for $100. At the aforementioned Wednesday meeting, there was no time to take up the clock matter, so Rosenheim told Lundy not to worry and convened a special Saturday morning meeting in his own office of the Municipal Art Commission where the clock plans were approved. On February 19, the Board of Public Works received the approved plans signed by commissioner members John W. Mitchell, president, and Alfred Rosenheim, secretary. The Board of Public Works then gave the "go ahead" for the clock's installation based on the Art Commission approval.

When Lundy later went to the Board of Public Works to receive his permit, he relayed the story of how his approval was granted to public works commissioner Hugh J. McGuire. McGuire became incensed at how the approval had been obtained and said he would speak with Mayor Meredith P. Snyder (1919–21) about what he claimed was a "hold-up" by Rosenheim.

When Rosenheim was confronted with the allegations, he stated, "It is true that I was retained as architect for the clock for the Italian Jewelry Company. It is true that the plans were laid before the Municipal Art Commission. I did not vote on the approval, however, I see nothing improper in my actions."[198]

Two days later, the city council saw things differently. The city council called Mayor Snyder to testify and asked if Rosenheim's actions made him liable for "criminal prosecution." No answer to that question was determined by Snyder or the council, but the council unanimously agreed with Mayor Snyder, who stated that Rosenheim had used his public office to "benefit himself financially by personal interest in matters coming under his jurisdiction."[199] Once everyone agreed on that point, the council voted to dismiss Rosenheim from the Municipal Art Commission.

During the council's meeting, other facts emerged regarding what occurred at the Saturday morning meeting in Rosenheim's office. Art Commission president John W. Mitchell stated only three members of the commission were at the meeting: Rosenheim, building inspector Backus and himself. Mitchell stated that Rosenheim and Backus voted for the clock's approval and he voted against. Mitchell said he voted against it because he was against all sidewalk clocks. After the vote, Mitchell requested that

Rosenheim remove his name, as the clock's designer, before the plans were submitted to the Board of Public Works, and Rosenheim did.

One of the councilmen in attendance, Bert L. Farmer, asked if the clock's approval was legal since the Art Commission's charter requires a quorum of six to approve actions. Farmer went on to say, "Mr. Mitchell has been very active in criticizing the Council for asserted failure to obey the law and the charter. Let us find out if the commission has been obeying the law in permitting three of its members to act as a committee and pass on plans and affix the indorsement of the commission to them."[200]

Rosenheim's response to all of this was, in part,

> *My prompt removal by Mayor Snyder without a hearing is in line with the petty politics at present being played at the city hall in anticipation of the coming city election. I have been identified with the art commission for more than ten years first as member, then president and latterly secretary, and have given much time to its duties with free and unlimited professional advice to its lay members, and can conscientiously claim to have been consistent and loyal to the city's interests at all times. I care nothing for the office, because it involves the expenditure of valuable time for which there is no remuneration. The only regret I feel is the manner of my retirement, which, very naturally, I would have preferred to be a voluntary move on my part.* [Signed] *A. F. Rosenheim.*[201]

Two weeks later, Rosenheim was suspended from the Southern California chapter of the American Institute of Architects for this offense. This must have been tough for Rosenheim to deal with since he had been a past president of the AIA and instrumental in the development of the Southern California chapter. Rosenheim was not prosecuted by the city attorney. His ouster and public downfall must have been deemed punishment enough.

Rosenheim's wife, Frances Wheelock Rosenheim, died at the age of seventy on April 23, 1931. Four years later, in June 1935, Alfred Rosenheim, seventy-five, married the boarder he and his wife had lived with for over a decade, Ruth Salmons, fifty-nine. The newlyweds would have eight years of married life together.

Rosenheim died on September 9, 1943, from heart disease. He was eighty-four years old. Ruth was his only survivor. The home Rosenheim built on Westchester Place is well known to certain TV viewers, and many of them have made it a pilgrimage site since it was memorably used in the first season of the television series *American Horror Story.*

Alfred Rosenheim Westchester Place home. *Courtesy of* The Brickbuilder.

Alfred Rosenheim Westchester Place home. *Courtesy of* The Brickbuilder.

NOTES

Chapter 1

1. Adams, *John D. Spreckles*, 287.
2. *Los Angeles Times*, September 13, 1908.
3. *Los Angeles Times*, June 8, 1909.
4. *San Diego Union*, July 20, 1910.
5. Ibid.
6. *The Evening Tribune*, October 1, 1910.
7. *San Diego Weekly Union*, October 20, 1910.
8. *Los Angeles Times*, December 11, 1910.
9. Ibid.
10. Adams, *John D. Spreckels*, 296–97.
11. *San Diego Union*, January 1, 1912.
12. *San Diego Union*, August 24, 1912.
13. *San Diego Union*, August 23, 1912.
14. Ibid.
15. *The San Diego Union*, August 24, 1912.
16. *Evening Tribune*, August 22, 1912.
17. Ibid.
18. Ed Fletcher Papers, 1870–1955, MSS.81, Box: 10 Folder: 11, General correspondence–Hartke, C.H., The Library, UC San Diego.
19. Ed Fletcher Papers, 1870–1955, MSS.81, Box: 1 Folder: 2, General correspondence–Albright, Mr. and Mrs. Harrison, The Library, UC San Diego.

Chapter 2

20. *Los Angeles Herald*, August 19, 1902.
21. *Notables of the Southwest*, 71.
22. Harper, ed., *Who's Who*, 23.
23. John C. Austin, "The Profession of Architecture," *Architect and Engineer* 30, no. 2 (August 1912): 49–50.
24. *Los Angeles Times*, August 26, 1922.
25. Al Malaikah, *Civic Need Fulfilled*.
26. *Los Angeles Times*, June 1, 1925.
27. *Los Angeles Times*, June 20, 1925.
28. Ibid.
29. "Allied Architects Association formed for the Advancement of Public Architecture," *Southwest Builder and Contractor* 58, no. 2 (July 8, 1921): 10–11.
30. Ibid.
31. *Los Angeles Times*, March 7, 1925.
32. Ibid.
33. Hales, *Los Angeles City Hall*, 63.
34. *Los Angeles Times*, March 27, 1928.
35. *Los Angeles Times*, February 6, 1935.
36. *Los Angeles Times*, September 5, 1903.
37. *Los Angeles Times*, September 5, 1903.
38. Ibid.
39. Ibid.
40. *Los Angeles Times*, October 12, 1931.
41. *Los Angeles Times*, November 16, 1931.
42. *Los Angeles Times*, September 12, 1934.
43. *Los Angeles Times*, November 26, 1934.
44. Ibid.
45. *Los Angeles Times*, March 1, 1935.
46. *Los Angeles Times*, March 17, 1935.
47. Ibid.
48. The Jonathan Club was an exclusive men's club founded in 1894 when the city's population was approximately fifty thousand. It was a social club whose members included prominent civic leaders and the city's top businessmen. In a phone conversation with the head of the membership committee at the Jonathan Club, it was explained that if members did not renew their membership or died, those current members in good standing had their

membership numbers advanced forward to a lower membership number. Austin was able to acquire the number one membership slot by paying his dues on time and outliving everyone else who had joined before him.

Chapter 3

49. *Lima News*, May 31, 1955.
50. Ibid.
51. Wolfe, *Men of California*, 227.
52. *Los Angeles Times*, March 9, 1924.
53. *Los Angeles Times*, October 27, 1924.
54. *Los Angeles Times*, May 2, 1926.
55. Ibid.
56. *Los Angeles Times*, May 13, 1926.
57. *Los Angeles Times*, December 16, 1928.
58. Ibid.
59. *Los Angeles Times*, June 1, 1930.
60. *Los Angeles Times*, March 29, 1931.
61. Ibid.
62. *Los Angeles Times*, September 12, 1930.
63. Ibid.
64. Ibid.
65. Ibid.
66. Personal conversation with Mr. Sieroty on August 7, 2017.
67. Ibid.
68. Ibid.
69. *Los Angeles Times*, February 2, 1963.

Chapter 4

70. Elmer Grey, "Vicissitudes of a Young Architect," *Architect and Engineer* 111, no. 2 (November 1932): 49–51.
71. Ibid.
72. Ibid.
73. Ibid.
74. Elmer Grey, "Vicissitudes of a Young Architect," *Architect and Engineer* 111, no. 3 (December 1932): 35–37.

75. *Pasadena Star News*, August 18, 1957.

76. Elmer Grey, "Vicissitudes of a Young Architect," *Architect and Engineer* 112, no. 1 (January 1933): 41–42.

77. *Pasadena Star News*, August 18, 1957.

78. Ibid.

79. Elmer Grey, "Vicissitudes of a Young Architect," *Architect and Engineer* 112, no. 2 (February 1933): 43–45.

80. Ibid.

81. *Los Angeles Times*, May 14, 1911.

82. Ibid.

83. Elmer Grey, "On the Design of Certain Modern Church Edifices," *Architectural Record* 34, no. 6 (December 1913): 544–56.

84. Ibid.

85. *Christian Science Sentinel*, February 28, 1914.

86. *Pasadena Star News*, August 18, 1957.

87. MacKaye, *Playhouse and the Play*, 79.

88. *Los Angeles Times*, February 9, 1924.

89. Ibid.

90. *Los Angeles Times*, September 28, 1924.

91. *Los Angeles Times*, May 18, 1925.

92. *Los Angeles Times*, April 26, 1925.

93. Ibid.

94. *Los Angeles Times*, May 20, 1925.

95. Elmer Grey, "Vicissitudes of a Young Architect," *Architect and Engineer* 114, no. 2 (August 1933): 31–33.

96. Ibid.

97. Ibid.

Chapter 5

98. *Los Angeles Times*, April 21, 1905.

99. *Los Angeles Times*, January 14, 1902.

100. *Los Angeles Herald*, July 23, 1905.

101. *Los Angeles Herald*, October 14, 1906.

102. *Los Angeles Times*, December 28, 1906.

103. *Los Angeles Times*, November 22, 1908.

104. Ibid.

105. *Los Angeles Times*, December 10, 1907.

106. *Los Angeles Times*, March 22, 1908.
107. Ibid.
108. *Los Angeles Times*, February 5, 1911.
109. Ibid.
110. *Los Angeles Times*, May 23, 1911.
111. Ibid.
112. *Los Angeles Times*, April 17, 1910.
113. *Los Angeles Herald*, August 20, 1911.
114. Ibid.
115. Ibid.
116. *Los Angeles Times*, June 21, 1911.

Chapter 6

117. George Credle, "Claud Beelman's Corporate Modern Style 1951–1963" (master's thesis, University of Southern California, 2012), 9.
118. Linda G. Arntzenius, "Architects of Early Twentieth Century Los Angeles and Their Legacy" (master's thesis, University of Southern California, 1998), 85–88.
119. *Notables of the Southwest*, 231.
120. *Los Angeles Times*, April 22, 1911.
121. *Los Angeles Herald*, April 23, 1911.
122. *Los Angeles Times*, December 30, 1916.
123. *Los Angeles Times*, January 27, 1918.
124. Ibid.
125. *Los Angeles Times*, December 23, 1917.
126. Ibid.
127. *Los Angeles Times*, February 2, 1918.
128. Ibid.
129. *Los Angeles Times*, March 28, 1928.
130. Kanner, *AC Martin Partners*, 34.
131. McDevitt, ed., *Courthouses of California*, 314.
132. *Los Angeles Times*, April 10, 1960.

Chapter 7

133. *Los Angeles Herald*, March 11, 1919.

134. *Los Angeles Times*, February 2, 1922.

135. *Los Angeles Times*, December 16, 1923.

136. *Los Angeles Times*, September 14, 1924.

137. *Los Angeles Times*, October 3, 1926. Note: Bernard V. Gerow, Harold F. Wilson and Louis Ghiloni were the architectural sculptors for the Chinese Theater.

138. *Los Angeles Times*, March 13, 1927.

139. *Los Angeles Times*, May 15, 1927.

140. *Los Angeles Times*, May 22, 1927.

141. *Los Angeles Times*, May 19, 1927.

142. *Los Angeles Times*, May 21, 1927.

143. *Los Angeles Times*, July 24, 1927.

144. *Los Angeles Times*, October 2, 1927.

145. *Los Angeles Times*, November 20, 1927.

146. *Los Angeles Times*, July 1, 1928.

147. *Los Angeles Times*, May 8, 1932.

Chapter 8

148. *San Francisco Chronicle*, December 8, 1901.

149. Ibid.

150. Richey, *Eminent Women of the West*, 245.

151. Patricia Failing, "She Was America's Most Successful Woman Architect," *Artnews* 80, no. 1 (January 1981): 66–71.

152. *Pasadena Star-News*, May 17, 1978.

153. *Los Angeles Times*, March 8, 1913.

154. It is unclear who oversaw the ceremony. The *Construction News* says Ingold. The *Los Angeles Times* says Wagner. It is possible they divided the master of ceremonies duties.

155. *Los Angeles Times*, August 12, 1913.

156. Ibid.

157. *Construction News*, January 24, 1914.

158. "Proposed Group for the YWCA of Pasadena, California," *California Southland* 14, no. 12 (December 1920): 12.

159. Relayed to the author in an email from Bharne on May 23, 2018.

160. *Los Angeles Times*, October 12, 1917.

161. *Los Angeles Times*, February 19, 1926.

Chapter 9

162. *Los Angeles Times*, July 31, 1896.

163. *Los Angeles Times*, April 25, 1905.

164. Octavius Morgan, "Architect's Morgans Views," *Architect and Engineer* 16, no. 3 (April 1909): 84.

165. *Los Angeles Times*, February 21, 1909.

166. *Los Angeles Times*, March 27, 1910.

167. According to the 1900 census.

168. *Los Angeles Times*, January 8, 1911.

169. Ibid.

170. *Los Angeles Times*, July 7, 1912.

171. *Los Angeles Herald*, February 7, 1913.

172. Ibid.

173. *Los Angeles Herald*, July 12, 1913.

174. Ibid.

175. *Los Angeles Times*, October 24, 1914.

176. Ibid.

177. *San Francisco Call*, September 25, 1913.

178. Ibid.

179. *Los Angeles Times*, January 20, 1922.

180. "Morgan, Walls & Clements," *Architect and Engineer* 51, no. 2 (May 1930): 27.

181. Harris Allen, "Terra Cotta Versus Terra Firma," *California Arts and Architecture* 37 no. 2 (February 1930): 32–39.

182. *Los Angeles Times*, March 22, 1987.

183. *Los Angeles Times*, January 24, 1929.

184. The Pellissier Building was declared Los Angeles Historic Cultural Monument No. 118 on May 16, 1973. The Bank of Italy Building was declared Los Angeles Historic Monument No. 354 on April 26, 1988. The Mayan Theater was declared Los Angeles Historic Cultural Monument No. 460 on October 17, 1989. The Chouinard Institute of Arts was declared Los Angeles Historic Cultural Monument No. 454 on October 24, 1989. The Belasco Theater was declared Los Angeles Historic Cultural Monument No. 476 on January 30, 1990. The El Capitan Theater Building was declared Los Angeles Historic Cultural Monument No. 495 on June 12, 1990.

185. *Los Angeles Times*, January 30, 1955.

186. *Los Angeles Times*, August 18, 1954.

187. *Los Angeles Times*, June 22, 1957.
188. *Los Angeles Times*, March 27, 1957.

Chapter 10

189. Alfred F. Rosenheim, "Half Century of Architectural Practice," *Architect and Engineer* 136, no. 4 (April 1939): 39–43.
190. *Los Angeles Times*, August 27, 1902.
191. Herman Hellman owned a building (a former home) that sat on the property where the Hellman building was to rise. According to the *Los Angeles Herald*, the Hellman building was not demolished, as other buildings on the site were; instead, Hellman's former home was moved to land that Hellman owned on the corner of Flower and Pico Streets.
192. Crandall, *Homage to Downtown*, 260.
193. Alfred F. Rosenheim, "Steel Frame the Safest Method of Building Construction," *Architect and Engineer* 14, no. 1 (August 1908): 49–51.
194. "Reinforced Concrete in Handsome Church at Los Angeles," *Concrete* 9, no. 3 (March 1, 1909): 75.
195. Fernand Parmentier, "Southern California Meeting Minutes," *American Institute of Architects Quarterly Bulletin* 12 no. 4 (January 1912): 296.
196. *Los Angeles Times*, February 24, 1921.
197. Ibid.
198. Ibid.
199. *Los Angeles Herald*, February 24, 1921.
200. *Los Angeles Times*, February 26, 1921.
201. *Los Angeles Herald*, February 25, 1921.

BIBLIOGRAPHY

Adams, H. Austin. *The Man: John D. Spreckels.* San Diego: Frye & Smith, 1924.

Allen, Harris. "Terra Cotta Versus Terra Firma." *California Arts and Architecture* 37, no. 2 (February 1930): 32–39.

Al Malaikah Company. *A Civic Need Fulfilled.* Los Angeles: Western Lithograph Co., 1925.

American Institute of Architects Quarterly Bulletin, various years.

Architect and Engineer, various years.

Arntzenius, Linda G. "Architects of Early Twentieth Century Los Angeles and Their Legacy." Master's thesis, USC, 1998.

Burdette, Robert J., ed. *Greater Los Angeles & Southern California Portraits & Personal Memoranda.* Los Angeles: Lewis Publishing Company, 1910.

California Southland, various years.

Christian Science Sentinel, various years.

Concrete, various years.

Crandall, John. *Homage to Downtown.* Sacramento, CA: Visions of LA, 2010.

Credle, George. "Claud Beelman's Corporate Modern Style 1951-1963." Master's thesis, USC, 2012.

Ed Fletcher papers, UC San Diego.

Failing, Patricia. "She was America's Most Successful Woman Architect." *Artnews* 80, no. 1 (January 1981): 66–71.

Gebhard, David. *The Richfield Building 1928–1968.* Los Angeles: Atlantic Richfield Co., 1970.

Guinn, J.M. *History of California and an Extended History of Los Angeles and Environs.* Los Angeles: Historical Record Company, 1915.

Bibliography

Hales, George P. *Los Angeles City Hall.* Los Angeles: Times Mirror Printing, 1928.

Harper, Franklin, ed., *Who's Who on the Pacific Coast.* Los Angeles: Harper Publishing Co., 1913.

Kanner, Diane. *AC Martin Partners: One Hundred Years of Architecture.* Los Angeles: AC Martin Partners, 2006.

Lima, Ohio News, various years.

Los Angeles Herald, various years.

Los Angeles Times, various years.

MacKaye, Percy. *The Playhouse and the Play.* New York: Johnson Reprint Corp., 1970.

McDevitt, Ray, ed. *Courthouses of California.* San Francisco: California Historical Society, 2001.

Men of the Pacific Coast. San Francisco: Pacific Art Co., 1903

Notables of the Southwest. Los Angeles: Los Angeles Examiner, 1913.

Pasadena Star News, various years.

Richey, Eleanor. *Eminent Women of the West.* Berkeley: Howell North Books, 1975.

Saint Vincent's. Los Angeles: Southland Publishing House, Inc., 1930.

San Diego Tribune, various years.

San Francisco Call, various years.

San Francisco Chronicle, various years.

Southwest Builder and Contractor, various years.

Wolfe, Wellington C. *Men of California.* San Francisco: Western Press Reporter, Inc., 1926.

Year Book: Los Angeles Architectural Club. 1910. Los Angeles: Geo. Rice & Sons.

Year Book: Los Angeles Architectural Club. 1911. Los Angeles: Cadmus Press.

Year Book: Los Angeles Architectural Club. 1912. Los Angeles: Kingsley, Mason & Collins.

Year Book: Los Angeles Architectural Club. 1913. Los Angeles: Kingsley, Mason & Collins.

INDEX

U

U.S. Grant Hotel 12, 13, 14, 16, 17

V

Van Dine, Julia
  second wife of W.A.O. Munsell 76
Van Nuys Hotel 148
Ventura County Courthouse 89, 101
Vidor, King 113, 114

W

Walls, John A. 128, 148
Walter P. Story Building 134
Wattles Mansion 57
Welton Becket & Associates 159
Wendt, Julia Bracken 84
West Baden Springs Hotel 12
Westchester Place
  home 167, 171, 174
Wheelock, Frances Graham
  wife of Alfred F. Rosenheim 161
Wilde, Louis J. 16, 17
Wollett, William L. 91
Workman, Boyle 29, 31
Wright & Callendar Building 113

Z

Zeiss 38, 40

ABOUT THE AUTHOR

Antonio Gonzalez is a resident of Los Angeles. He has a BA in journalism from the University of Iowa, a MLIS from San Jose State University and is currently enrolled in the Heritage Conservation program at USC. He is a member of the Odd Fellows fraternity, works in an architecture and fine arts library and has a blog where he posts items related to architecture and his other interests. His blog can be found at misterdangerous.wordpress.com.